# A THIRST FOR MEANING

# A THIRST FOR MEANING

in the face of skepticism and doubt

by CALVIN MILLER

*16377*

**ZONDERVAN**
**PUBLISHING HOUSE**
OF THE ZONDERVAN CORPORATION
GRAND RAPIDS, MICHIGAN 49506

A THIRST FOR MEANING
Copyright © 1973, 1976 by The Zondervan Corporation
Grand Rapids, Michigan
Second printing (First Zondervan Books Edition) 1976
Library of Congress Catalog Card Number 73-2656

*Printed in the United States of America*

# CONTENTS

# PREFACE

Reason is sometimes a bully. He shoves and pushes his way into Christian conversation and shames our faith. He grins at the shallowness of the faithful, and accuses them of intellectual bankruptcy. He hears us speaking our creeds and mocks our simple devotion. He sits through the testimonies of salvation and says with belittling arrogance, "Is that all there is?"

And often the faithful crawl away and huddle over creeds they do not have the wisdom to defend. To the cynics, Christians appear to own nothing and our Hope in Christ looks small and of no importance.

This book has for its sole purpose a desire to help you stand up. The skeptics would be amazed at how tall you really are, if you would but stand. You need not cower before the intellectual onslaughts of Christianity's assassins. You are a believer. You are the chosen. You have a destiny to live out. You have drunk from the eternal purposes of God and you are full. It is the skeptics glutted with their logic who are really hungry.

But merely to stand is not enough. You must stand in love. It is not to your advantage to trade blows with intellectuals. This is no crude, cold war we must win to establish our position. It is merely our attempt to stop groveling before the cynics.

I urge you gently but firmly to stand in the council of antagonists, to throw your chest out, and speak above their chilling cries. Say to them, "Come with me, all you who doubt." You may even use the invitation of Isaiah, "Ho, everyone that thirsteth, come ye to the waters . . . ." And you may do it with the sure knowledge that the skeptic is more ready to listen than he seems. For he is possessed of a desperate thirst for meaning.

# CHAPTER ONE

Will they never learn? The man who comes
with the bread of pity and the bread of life in
his hands is doomed, forever and a day, on
Terra, to hatred and assassination.

TAYLOR CALDWELL
*Dialogues with the Devil*

# A CARPENTER'S REASON

YOUR conversion was a splendid moment of inheritance. When you opened your life to Christ, it became a treasury of truth. When you breathed the words, "Yes, Lord," Jesus Christ, the most valuable object of our Heavenly Father's esteem, was enclosed inside your soul. At that moment you became heir to the entire estate of God. And the earnest of your inheritance, which you are shortly to be given, is the Truth.

There is only one thing of real value about your life — the indwelling Truth. Jesus Christ is the personal truth of God. He exists in your life, which is set in a world that is most uncertain. You always encounter in other persons the possibility of error or falsehood. Dare we say: "The universe has been subverted by Satan, the father of falsehood. Men lie." They lie in the marketplace, haggling over brass they represent as gold. We sometimes buy. They lie at great tables of armistice. Then shortly we go to war again. They perjurethemselves in courts. They lie on star-spangled political platforms.

They lie even to you. But, you may not judge your dishonest world too quickly for even you have lied. Simply, perhaps — in some little way. Yet you have made your contribution to universal falsehood. But do not despair. The lie is all-pervasive. It started in Eden, and the shot ricocheted throughout creation. No soul was safe or exempt after Adam.

11

Error became the principle of humanity in revolt against God. So you were doomed in the book of Genesis to live with the principle of the lie.

But here is precisely the glory of human redemption from sin. God in Christ dealt with the lie. He overcame it with a powerful truth that could live in a spoiled universe. This truth was so dynamic that it was not intimidated or extinguished even by Satan himself. Not that he has not tried. Of course he has. He knows the truth of God will ultimately smash his negative, two-faced stranglehold on Adam's children.

Therefore, truth is the only value or victory there is. In becoming a Christian you agree not merely to become the receptacle of truth, but also to be its guardian. Thus your conversion was *your* decision to no longer participate in the lie. You gave your entire consent for the Truth to move into both your life and your life-style. And at that majestic moment of repentance you confessed the lie to which you had given your consent for numbers of years. You may even have wept at your allegiance to falsehood. You repudiated worthless living and agreed that the only real worth was Jesus Christ, the eternal truth of God. And the unspeakable treasures of redemption were yours.

You understood that there was no intrinsic worth in you personally. Men admire treasure and not treasure chests; cash and not money clips; currency and not money bags. The container was ever second to the contents. What you possessed was of value. Your own personality was but the "canister" of truth you had become in Christ.

Since this inner truth is the greatest and most valuable of all your assets, you must safeguard it just as you would all your other possessions: your family, home or auto. As the word "rapist" threatens the sanctity of your family, as the word "burglar" threatens the security of your home, so the word "lie" should threaten you and rally all your defenses around the priceless inner truth that is yours.

If you wish a standard for measuring the value of the indwelling Christ, you must study those who paid for their faith with their blood. The martyrs afford the clearest example of those who most dearly valued the truth. Those who were often the outcasts of the slave economy knew its magnificent worth. Most of them could have avoided execution by merely calling the truth a lie. Yet they clung tenaciously to the inner reality when burning a pinch of incense to the Emperor would have freed them.

For that matter, Christ Himself could have avoided death by saying simply, "I was mistaken, Pilate, I am not the Christ!" But when He was asked if He were the "King of the Jews," His reply was quiet but affirmative. So He died, when the tiniest lie would have saved Him. Of course, Christ was a Trustee of Truth also. He was, in fact, the first. The martyrs who came later were but the echoes of His faithful trust, keeping for themselves exactly what He kept for Himself — that supreme integrity, which to surrender is to destroy.

How did we come to view so casually what they viewed so earnestly? We seem to be playing the same game as the martyrs with an entirely different rule book. But then, Christians are living in the Green Zone now — they are safe to believe. They are even congratulated for doing so. The martyrs were not congratulated for believing — they were executed. But we are intimidated by smaller threats. We retreat before the fear of little reprisals and will not speak in defense of the great Truth we contain.

Our reason is faulty. We need to adopt the attitude of Christ, who pronounced a benediction upon all who were "persecuted for righteousness' sake" (Matt. 5:10). He cautioned us to remember that in defending the truth we should not be alarmed before our accusers for "it shall be given you in that same hour what ye shall speak" (Matt. 10:19). Paul, operating by the reason of Christ, encouraged all to be bold in "the acknowledging of the truth" (2 Tim. 2:25; Titus 1:1).

13

This truth of which you are a trustee emerged suddenly in Nazareth of Galilee. No sooner had the truth been stated than its antithesis was shouted into existence. The antithesis to the "Truth" is the "Lie." The Lie obviously contends that the Truth is not so. The two sprang into being almost at one time, and they have survived the centuries together — the Truth and the Lie. The Truth has faithfully affirmed the divinity of Christ; the Lie has consistently denied it. Still the quarrel lives on. For a moment, let us return to the wellspring of this long-standing struggle.

The whole thing might have seemed a teapot tempest to most of us. At the time it probably would have appeared to be a prosaic, synagogue debate. But the feud was earnest. At the eye of the storm was a Rabbi, newly ordained by the sun and the fields and — above all — ordained by His God.

He had come home.

The furor that met His homecoming was prompted by a contemptible familiarity. They knew Him. In fact, quite well! But His townsmen never knew the vast reality that existed beyond their little worlds of understanding. They illustrate that mere human knowledge is confining; to "know" is often to bind with little definitions. It is to reason: "I know the Golden Gate Bridge; I cross it twice each day. It has two piers and two cables. I have always known it that way, and therefore, it can be no other. Not the cleverest logician can temper what I know by an extra foot of cable."

Jesus was known. He was so tall and of a certain appearance: hazel-eyed, stout-faced, callus-handed. His face and mannerisms were part of the community. So it was unthinkable that this Jesus should stand on a normal sun-baked Sabbath and say:

> The Spirit of the Lord is upon me, because he hath anointed me to preach the gospel to the poor; he hath sent me to heal the brokenhearted, to preach deliverance to the captives, and recovering of sight to the blind, to set at liberty them that are bruised, To preach the acceptable year of the Lord (Luke 4:18, 19).

14

Could this be the village timberdresser? Joseph's boy? Yes, of course, it was. And they had called Him Carpenter too long ever to call Him Christ. "Jesus Carpenter" they could speak. "Jesus Christ" stuck in their throats.

In Nazareth they made Him choose the smaller modifier: Jesus, son of Joseph, not Son of God; Jesus, Carpenter, not Christ.

The predicament of the Nazarenes is not that they knew Him too well, but that they did not know Him at all. "I am the Christ!" He said. "No, you are the Carpenter," said they. "No, I am *a* Carpenter, but I am *the* Christ." "Rather *a* carpenter, only! Joseph's boy! We know you."

Well, that is enough space to give the long-dead opponents of Jesus. The Christ is yet alive, and those in His generation who thought Him only a Carpenter are gone. But the controversy about Jesus still rages. Some still think Him only a carpenter and some the Christ. In every era those who hear of Him align themselves one way or the other. Nero, Voltaire, and Bertrand Russell thought Him only a Carpenter; Paul, Augustine, and Billy Sunday believed Him the Christ.

The unusual thing about the debate is that there is no middle way. There were none in Nazareth who said, "Maybe Carpenter, maybe Christ!" On this issue everyone still takes one side or the other.

One other thing is worthy of notice: the rigid view of the Carpenter School. One would expect the "Jesus-is-Christ" camp to affirm their position insistently. But it is often a surprise to see the other wing affirming with equal vehemence, "This is Joseph's boy, the Carpenter!" This is especially interesting so many years after the fact.

Why don't the dissenters merely affirm their position and seek out some more meaningful argument? But no! They seem to feel an irrepressible need to proclaim His Carpentry. A negative compulsion forces them to refute His Godhood, and to be zealously evangelistic about it.

They are as sincere as they are zealous. If you ask them the *why's* of their negative evangelism, they will tell you their concern for a Carpenter Theology is in the interest of "enlightenment" or "intellectual honesty" or "the advance of pure reason." But their zeal often leads the observer to conclude their need to be right is intense. No one, it seems, hungers for converts quite so much as a militant atheist.

Christians call Jesus "Christ," because they have exercised "faith" and been filled with "truth." The Carpenterians, on the other hand, have applied "logic" and are filled with "fact." The Carpenterian's credo runs something like this: "Is it logical that a Carpenter could be the Christ, the Son of God?" The answer is "no." Therefore, His Carpentry is established on the basis of sound reason.

The Christian conversely says, "I believe He is the Christ!" By this confession truth is appropriated and "interiorized" in the believer.

When the debate begins, Christians and Carpenterians always fight with very different weapons. The former bring their Bibles, visions, and experiences and say, "Now see here." The latter bring their slide rules, historians, and philosophers and say, "You were saying!" When the battle is over, the debate seems to have been a draw. Only infrequently does a Christian abandon his faith for the logic of the Carpenterians. And perhaps just as infrequently will a dyed-in-the-wool Carpenterian trade his "facts" for the "truth" and become a Christian.

Occasionally a skeptic will protest that he has sought the Truth with an open mind but to no avail. Though he is sincere, it is usually obvious that he has not abandoned his presuppositions before he began his search. A scoffer may indeed long to have the Christian truth.

This kind of man using the wrong tools very much resembles Nietzsche's *Mad Man.* Remember how he came into the marketplace on a sunlit day, carrying a lantern, which he thrust into every darkened niche, and cried, "I seek God! I seek God!" Since he did not find God, he concluded that

16

God was dead and churches were nothing more than His tombs and sepulchres.

Forgive me if I deal harshly with a story that was clearly intended as a parable. Yet the *Mad Man* was using the wrong tools in his search. You do not track God with a lantern or a coil of rope. Facts are empirical; you may therefore use lanterns to discover them and ropes to bind them once they are discovered. But gospel truth is not apprehended by logic.

You contain the truth as a believer, but you do not possess the ability to rationally define what you own. Let us compare this Christian truth you have with love. When a man and a woman share a deep relationship, they are said to be "in love." Their love is real, but hardly empirical. They can think of no logical reason they feel as they do toward each other. The affair is not chemical or biological or animal or vegetable or mineral. By all rational principles, love shouldn't be and yet it is. The romantic lyricist can only describe this nonscientific state by crooning:

> I don't know why I love you like I do,
> I don't know why, I just do.

As a trustee of truth you also can say, "I don't know why this truth should be so great, but I know that it is." The answer to your dilemma is really not *un*reasonable, merely *beyond* reason.

Let's take an incident from the sixth chapter of John. The Jews were murmuring because Jesus claimed to be the bread come down from heaven. Then again comes the familiar argument:

> Is not this Jesus, the son of Joseph, whose father and mother we know? How is it then that he saith, I came down from heaven? (John 6:42)

It is not really illogical that he could be the Messiah (he is certainly someone great, for he has just divided the loaves among thousands), it is just beyond all logic.

But the conclusion of current Carpenterians, after they

have applied logical methods of inquiry, is that you as a Christian really do not own anything, because you cannot define it to their satisfaction. Your claim of possessing substantial truth is buried by their pleas for "real" evidence.

If the truth you possess is beyond all reason, how can you defend its reality or substance before rational onslaughts? The only way to reason convincingly is to reason from your own experience.

Let's go back to our illustration on love. Suppose you state there really is such a thing as love. If a skeptic asks you for objective evidence, you might protest that you are in love and know the condition to be real. You have all the symptoms. You offer these facts: you tingle when you are around a certain person; you perspire; you get butterflies in your stomach. Your opponent argues that none of those reactions are measurable phenomena. So you offer the evidence. You point to the lipstick on the collar or the engagement ring on your finger and say, "See, here is an evidence of love." "No," argues the skeptic, "these are only evidences of expenditure or cosmetics; they do not conclusively prove that a condition of love exists." (He would be right!) So you say, "Some day, you skeptic, you will fall in love and know that it really does exist."

Jesus defended the truth on the basis of His experience. His defense was "taste and see." Notice His argument after He had claimed to be the bread of heaven:

> I am that bread of life.
> Your fathers did eat manna in the wilderness, and are dead.
> This is the bread [he said gesturing to himself]
> which came down from heaven, that a man
> may eat thereof and not die.
> I am the living bread which came down from heaven:
> if any man eat of this bread, he shall live for ever.
>
> (John 6:48-51)

He told them that however unreasonable it sounded they only had to taste to see. Using the same reason, He invited the Samaritan woman to taste the Water of life and "see" if it would not forever quench her thirst.

Your experiences can be formidable foes even for the hard-line cynic. Remember the man born blind in the ninth chapter of John? His healing brought a controversy of some size into the council. Yet his experience with the truth included the phenomenon of sight. The skeptics encouraged him to praise God and not his healer who was a sinner.

> He answered and said, Whether he be a sinner or no, I know not: one thing I know, that, whereas I was blind, now I see (John 9:25).

The man, relying on his experience with the truth, made such a brilliant defense that his adversaries in anger cast him out.

Testimony has become the primary way Christians relate their experience. Paul tells his testimony four times in the book of Acts. Your experiences with the Truth will be hard to refute if they are accompanied by changes in behavior and love for others.

We are usually told that our experiences are too "common" to be respected by the skeptics. We seem to feel that a dramatic and supernatural experience is necessary to overwhelm the Carpenterians. We could use Paul's desert lightning, or Constantine's old *in hoc signo*. Or maybe we could borrow Elijah's fiery chariot to drive to philosophy class for just one day. . . .

While a few have "visions and revelations" to boast about, most of us must make our defense with less sophisticated equipment. Your experience may seem starkly plain. There will be no lightning bolt or flaming seraphim anywhere in your confession of faith.

Perhaps every Christian who has needed to defend his truth against the doubts of others, or against his own doubts, has pleaded for a sign — a bit of fire to hallow the humdrum. Like young John Bunyan, we would like to call down celestial fire to dry up mud puddles so we would have something of an impressive nature to report.

We know the kind of proof the skeptics ask for. They are like King Herod in *Jesus Christ Superstar* taunting Him for proof, asking Him to change water into wine. But Christ refused to give Herod a sign. He had given one to the people when He multiplied the loaves and the end product of that sign was stupefaction — not faith. So it would have been with Herod.

The absence of supernatural displays keeps Christianity from becoming a bargain-basement religion — a magician's hat of mystifying events that gets the "ooh's" and "ahh's" of a fireworks display. Such displays are always brilliant against a dark sky, but they are short-lived. Faded fireworks inevitably leave us in inky blackness trying to remember the form of the brief fiery etching.

Drama is unavailing as a force against skepticism anyway. To demonstrate this Jesus told the story of the rich man and Lazarus. The rich man in hell was torn by thoughts of his brothers who were yet alive. He petitioned Father Abraham to resurrect Lazarus, the beggar, and send him to his living kin to preach a sermon on the horrors of hell. The conversation went like this:

> *Abraham:* Son, remember that thou in thy lifetime receivedst thy good things, . . . likewise Lazarus evil things.
> *Rich Man:* I pray thee therefore, father, that thou wouldst send him to my father's house; for I have five brethren; that he may testify unto them, lest they also come to this place of torment.
> *Abraham:* They have Moses and the prophets; let them hear them.
> *Rich Man:* Nay, father Abraham: but if one went unto them from the dead, they will repent.
> *Abraham:* If they hear not Moses and the prophets, neither will they be persuaded, though one rose from the dead.

(Based on Luke 16:25-31.)

Let us suppose for a moment that Abraham granted his

20

wish and brought Lazarus back. Let us suppose the beggar stalked into the family reunion of the rich man's surviving relatives and said, "I bear you greetings from your brother. He is in hell. He screams in pitiless torment night and day. It is his wish that you sell your villas, wardrobes, and estates, that you give your properties to charity so you can avoid his eternal sufferings."

Would his kinsfolk have obeyed a resurrected Lazarus? It is doubtful. Ebenezer Scrooge is probably the only person converted to humanitarianism by the influence of spirits. Likely they would have argued like Scrooge that Lazarus's shade was a bit of "undigested beef" or an "old potato." They would have reminisced years later around the fireplace over the night they saw Old Lazarus at the family reunion. But would the apparition have changed them? Doubtfully. Their lives would still be centered around the acquisition of things just as their relative's life had been during his earthly existence. They never had heeded the sacred Scriptures, so the vision of a dead beggar would not have sobered them long.

Paul argues for the less dramatic but more productive communication of our experience. "Faith cometh by hearing, and hearing by the word of God" (Rom. 10:17). Defending the truth is best and most frequently done by using our own simple but meaningful experience. We may imagine that it would be easier if we could stretch out rods and divide the sea, while our adversaries focused their Polaroid cameras — but it would not.

People are more impressed with the practicality of a thing, anyway. We ought to be like the man born blind; we must understand that the practicality of an event demonstrates its worth more than the drama does. A simple man who had become a Christian was pursued by an intellectual critic who wanted to know exactly how Christ changed 120 gallons of water to wine. But the convert's concern in the issue was pragmatic. "I only know," he said, "that in my case, He did something far more practical — He changed beer into furniture." The "use" of the truth we keep is ultimately more impressive than the "wow" of it.

Thus, the Carpenter's Reason was a practical one. Christ did not want Christianity to become a doctrinal gallery where dogmas are displayed for consideration and debate. Christianity is to be a tool kit, a physician's case. Everything in the interest of good health is here. Here are the tools to treat the wounds of living: sterilizers for cleansing infected philosophies; Band-Aids for the little hurts of which life is made. The Sermon on the Mount is an expose of the practical nature of Christ's Reason. It is filled with suggestions on prayer, almsgiving, and freedom from hypocrisy. Even His initial statement of His Messiahship is a statement on how utterly practical and thus meaningful Christianity is to be: it liberates the captive; it cures the diseased; it guarantees the pursuit of happiness to the poor and the downtrodden.

Jesus' brother, James, had been a Carpenterian but after the resurrection became a Christian. His great argument in support of the Christian faith is a practical document. A Gospel which did not warm the naked and nourish the starving laid no real claim to authenticity. "Faith without works is dead," said James. An impractical philosophy is worthless, however intriguing it may be. The most convincing argument in favor of Christianity is the statement, "It works!" Better yet, "It works for me!" If we are hard-pressed to answer the question, "How does it work?" we can always point to the product.

Remember the king in the fable "Rumpelstiltskin"? It is enough for him that the daughter of the miller can spin straw into gold. He accepts her uncanny craft as a most practical and useful talent. He isn't even curious enough about the process to send a peeping Tom to the dungeon keyhole to see "how" the girl starts with bundles and ends with ingots. The "how" was unimportant to the king. There was a visible, spendable product, so her curious methods were of no importance.

22

The fact that there is product in Christianity will never be totally accepted. Some will always insist on the schematics of Atonement or want to wrangle over the inaccuracy of the shop manuals. Some will always be there to ask loudly, with those in Galilee, "Is this not the carpenter's son? How is it that he says, 'I am the bread come down from heaven'?"

Remember, the practical evidence that Jesus is Christ has already been displayed in Galilee. They are a starving, ragtag assembly. They are penniless peasants, but they eat this day. There is food for all, perhaps the first meal many of them have enjoyed in a long time. Because of the intense, usable, practical nature of Christianity, there is bread.

Once they are filled, they become philosophical. One can scarcely fail to notice that philosophy is the pastime of affluence. The hungry rarely have time for it. Great revivals of hope and humanism are born in times of repression and not seasons of abundance. Only after they have been warmed with bread and fish do men volley with cynicism. It is inconceivable that none believe — because of the utterly practical miracle of the loaves.

But the hard-core skeptic will rarely be convinced by practical confessions. He is basically a theoretician; argumentation is his greatest joy. Becoming a Christian is a threat to his life-style because it would eliminate the argument upon which his vicious mentality regularly feeds. His greatest triumph is in the siege of weaker intellects. And you provide the target he needs.

If you allow him to succeed, he will leave you convinced that your faith is nothing. On the basis of deductive reasoning he will denude your creed and destroy your miracles. If you will fight for the substance of your faith, do it as a well-trained soldier. Study the logic of your adversaries. Learn all you can about your opponents.

In the movie *Patton*, the American general deploys a trap for the enemy. Rommel and his *Afrika Korps* fall into the snare off guard and are defeated, and Hitler's African campaign is destroyed. As Patton looks over the battlefield, he says, "Aha, Rommel, I read your book. . . ."

We are always better able to deal with the enemy if we know his philosophy ahead of time. The twentieth century Christian cannot afford to be ignorant. Let us mature in faith, and learn the philosophies of our antagonists. As we become aware of the logic of the Lie, we will hold the Truth with greater security. This knowledge of the anti-Christian position may seldom help us convert our adversaries, but it will prevent us from being debilitated by their logic.

Jesus affirmed that He was the Truth and the Life. We who join the battle must realize the tradition which has preceded us. Our cry is, "Jesus is Christ." To those who yell back across the trenches, "No, he is Carpenter," we must point to the product of our position: peace, destiny, meaning. If they reply with pity for our superstitions, ask them for the product of their philosophy.

If they say their product is enlightenment, find out if it is frenzied. If they say their product is realism, ask if it is hungry realism. If they say it is honesty, ask if it is schizoid.

After such exchanges, they may not admit their absence of product, but this searching will give them a sense of our faith. When we have walked away from the duel, we might chance to see them looking wistfully over their shoulders for some more fertile hope. And occasionally one of them might say, "I believe. . . . Lord, help my unbelief."

You see, the Carpenterians are hungry. Right after they affirm that He is at the very most "Carpenter," they cry out hungrily, "Physician, heal yourself! Do in your hometown what you did in Capernaum" (from Luke 4:23). Those who hold the Truth as the Lie must always learn that there is little product in their skepticism. Their hunger for the supernatural will never bear fruit — not in Nazareth. For He cannot do ". . . many mighty works there because of their unbelief" (Matt. 13:58).

At the person of Christ, the road forks. Those on the barren

24

trail disappear over the horizon of time, muttering hungrily that He was only a Carpenter. There is only muttering on the logical road to doubt. But those on the other road move to drive a certain stake in a certain destiny. And ever and anon they stop and cry with overwhelming joy, "He is the Christ."

# CHAPTER TWO

*He raised his hand and over the desolate earth
he traced in space the sign of the dollar.*

AYN RAND
*Atlas Shrugged*

# TRUE STUFF

THE new materialism has vividly declined the universe. In all the whirling orbs and sparse gases there are only two kinds of items: things which own, and things which are owned. The owners of things are called "persons." The things which are owned are called "stuff." Now perhaps it seems unfair to resolve the universe with such radical simplicity. And it will have to be conceded that this brief definition of all matter is done totally by the mind of man himself.

Still, all stuff is molecular. The atomists tell us that all matter consists of some one hundred (plus) basic elements. That is to say that somewhere between actinium and zirconium there are a hundred elements out of which all things are made. Therefore the difference between an alligator bag and a block of ice, let us say, is the arrangement of neutrons, electrons, and what have you. So is it with all stuff.

Chemically we are ourselves a comedy. For while we do not consider ourselves stuff like all other stuff, we, too, are built out of basic elements, the organic ones: carbon, hydrogen, oxygen, nitrogen, with a trace of a half-dozen other elements thrown in. The comedy is this: that we, the organic elements, are the elements of ownership, while the inorganic elements constitute all that is owned. So this is the elemental picture: man, carbon-hydrogen-oxygen-nitrogen, lording it over everything else from aluminum to uranium. The former category is persons; the latter, stuff.

For the sake of clarity let it be said that man is not the only thing composed of organic elements. All life is. A cow, for instance. Yet man is the only organic item in the universe with a need to cry "mine." Thus he owns even organic stuff. He may own a cow or a borzoi or a colony of bees. And these organic things which belong to him he would classify as a part of his stuff. There have been long periods of human slavery when men owned other men; in these instances the slaves themselves were seen to be mere stuff, to be used or disposed of or sold like other stuff.

Nearly everyone seems possessed of a need to say, "This stuff is mine." Occasionally there is a Trappist monk or a guru who gives up all desire for stuff and appears to live his days as a stuffless person. But for most the picture is entirely opposite. One thinks of gluttonous kings surfeiting at banquet tables, gloating over all they own and bragging that all the substance between the river on the north and the mountains on the south is theirs. Or one remembers the conquistadors planting Spanish flags all over South America for Ferdinand and Philip and saying the appropriate Spanish words, the translation of which was "el stuffo."

Then there have always been wars for the boundaries — two or more great powers saying each to the other, "This land is mine," and others replying, "No, it is mine." Sometimes the battles for possession have raged for centuries, as in the case of the Arabs and the Jews warring for thirty-five hundred years over their Mediterranean real estate. Perhaps the most grandiose symbol of presumption and possessiveness is the planting of the American flag on the moon. While presumably we Americans would not say they own even lunar real estate, they would never permit any secondary flag-planters to say they owned it either.

So this is enough to mark out the categories of people and things. With the possible exception of oxygen, oceans, sunlight, and migratory birds, everything is either a possessor or a possession. Because of the close ties between persons and materials, few great philosophies have existed which did not concern man's relationships to stuff. Karl Marx, whose philosophies have deeply marked most of the world, taught that only by an equitable division of stuff among all peoples could life have meaning for all.

Is the only true stuff elemental? That is to ask, Is there any immaterial substance? Is there any valuable reality beyond physical demonstration?

Jesus' teachings on stuff are most interestingly unique. It is only His differentiation between stuff and non-stuff which may lead to ultimate fulfillment. Jesus taught that things are not as they appear. For those things that appear to be the most valuable of substance are subject to canker, decay, rust, and dissolution. True Stuff, rather, is not the tangible and marketable possession. In fact, you might acquire true stuff only in certain instances by "selling all you have" (see Matt. 19: 21). Christ taught in His Sermon on the Mount that true stuff may not be labeled "mine" and stacked in safety-deposit boxes. The real possessions are laid up beyond the planet (Matt. 6:20; Luke 12:21), for all earthly material is cankered (James 5:3). Jesus' climactic illustration on the nature of true stuff was the rich fool (Luke 12:20ff.), who amassed an earthly fortune but departed life without any real goods.

In the Old Testament it was not man who owned things, but God. The earth was the Lord's (Ps. 24:1), and the cattle on a thousand hills did not belong to the rancher but to God (Ps. 50:10). God created all stuff (Gen. 1:1) out of nothing, ex *nihilo* as the theologians say. God as the stuff-maker was the stuff-owner. But by Christ's time men had gotten pretty possessive with God's stuff, so Jesus made His pronouncements about the nature of true stuff.

The values of the materialist revolution are set against Christian values. The materialists have said that real estate, stocks and bonds, mercantile items are the true stuff. "No," argues the Christ, "the spirit of man, his destiny, his ministry to need are the various units of true substance."

Capitalism has been aided in its veneration of stuff by the whole ecology movement. The supporters of better ecological control have varied the theme a little. They have implanted the concept that the earth is jointly owned by her inhabitants and thereby they minimize individual capital. Still, they have also venerated stuff as in imminent danger of death. World ownership dies with man. Therefore man must save the world for himself, which he can do only as he saves himself for his world.

Greed is stuff-hunger. And this greed not only has led us into lasciviousness with our resources, but also has raped the earth. Let it be said at this point that I am an avid supporter of ecology. I do not do it to be stylish in my selection of causes. Rather, I do it because I hunger to exist free of contamination and guarantee to my children that theirs may breathe pure air and drink pure water. Nonetheless, it is God's earth for which I fight and not mine. The earth is still the Lord's (Ps. 24:1); we have dirtied it, polluted it with oil slicks, poisoned its waters, but we have not changed its ownership. Nature is God's.

When ecologists tell us we must save the natural world from death, we must be careful lest in the intensity of their issue we become guilty of thinking that natural substance is the only substance there is. The continuation of the world is important to any thinking person, but the Christian must always remember that the earth is not the ultimate stuff. Christ made it quite clear that true stuff is not terrestrial, and nothing is to be profited by "gaining the whole world and losing our own soul" (see Matt. 16:26). No, there is something beyond the good earth with her sweet waters and warm soils.

The materialist spirit of every age has exalted what it considered true stuff. Certain metals: gold and silver. Certain stones: sapphires, rubies, diamonds, emeralds. But the metals and stones were considered the most valuable of stuff because they were the most rare. To possess a great deal of these rarer elements was supposed to give you substance; but it did not give you security or peace. It could not make you secure since there was always a number of bandits menacing your strongbox. It cannot give you peace since to own a few of the rare metals or stones builds a fiery hunger inside you to own more and more. Like drinking sea water, gaining each new acquisition only makes your thing-thirst more unmanageable.

To own material was (and indeed is) the most evident cause of suffering. It makes everyone suffer. The rich suffer from wanting more; the poor suffer from having less and craving more. As the song so well expressed it:

Ask the rich man he'll confess,
Money can't buy happiness,
Ask the poor man, he don't doubt,
That he'd rather be miserable with than without.

33

And this inequity of life to which Marx protested with legitimate protests has often built a grotesque world. It was a world where Venetian doges oppressed the poor and czars went home from the opera houses to their grand mansions through Moscow's intolerable slums.

But much of the world misery was caused by a lack of understanding as to the nature of what true stuff is. There is at the moment even a secular awakening to the bad values by which men have hoarded and hungered for stuff. While the new values are not Christian — in that they have not esteemed the soul or eternity as real things to be owned — they have at least decried the current greed in which people hunger after false values.

For instance Charles Lindbergh said,

> I grew up as a disciple of science. I know its fascination. I have felt the godlike power man derives from his machines. . . . Now I have lived to experience the early results of scientific materialism. I have watched men turn into human cogs in the factories they believed would enrich their lives. I have watched pride in workmanship leave and human character decline as efficiency of production lines increased. . . . We still have the possibility, here in America, of building a civilization based on Man, where the importance of an enterprise is judged less by its financial profits than by the kind of community it creates; where the measure of a man is his own character, not his power or wealth. [1]

Then, too, Charles A. Reich has said:

> Even a millionaire would in actual fact be "better off" if he chose liberation instead of the plastic world of material wealth. If he exchanged wealth, status and power for love, creativity and liberation, he would be far happier; he would "make a good bargain." [2]

34

It goes without saying that if there are values beyond the material just from a secular viewpoint, how much greater are the non-material values about which Jesus talked.

Christ established His church to preach His values. The church was to keep straight on what really did constitute true stuff. At the outset of this part of the discussion, let it be firmly noted that the church was not (and is not) a building. The church is people. Confessedly, in our day when most hear the word "church," they conjure up an image of a gilded temple, expensively constructed of stuff. With her emphasis on expanded budgets and pledge drives and imported fixtures, the church has not been able to say with a great deal of meaning, "The soul of man is the true stuff."

The Water of Life is the true stuff (see John 4), but it is an intangible, and the church has majored on the Ornate Waterworks. Church houses have tended to become shrines, often expensive in their decor, and when they say we are in business for a penniless Carpenter, their grand budgets belie their values. In honor of her poor founder the church has driven elegant sanctuaries into the earth.

The church has affirmed that human redemption is true stuff, while her board of investors has bought apartment complexes, football stadiums, and available stocks and bonds. Indeed, very few churches are able to say with the Apostle Peter in the first century, "Silver and gold have I none." So in the materialistic revolution the church has appeared blatantly false.

In James Michener's Hawaii, the John Whipple family arrive in the islands to practice compassion and soon see how the islands (and they themselves) could profit from a general store. Within a few generations the Whipples own their share of holdings in the islands,

35

and their noble idealism of teaching the heathen of true stuff has gone by the board.

The church often appears this way in the midst of her materialistic critics. I have heard it said that when the Communists were meeting in Russia to decide how to take over the world, the bishops were meeting down the street to decide what colors their vestments ought to be for the various litanies. One wonders what the bishops preached after they had decided which of their costly vestments to wear. Could it possibly be that in their ermine-trimmed capes they told the student rabble that the Bolsheviks sinned in seeking the material, when, after all, the true stuff was spiritual?

In our own country the church has often catered a strange brand of Calvinism. Adam Smith, that delightful alias who wrote *The Money Game*, said:

> Bishop Lawrence . . . was J. P. Morgan's preacher, and of a Sunday he would look down at the assembled Wall Street tycoons in individually endowed pews and say, "Godliness is in league with riches; it is only to the moral man that wealth comes. Material prosperity makes the nation sweeter, more joyous, more unselfish, more Christlike." [3]

Smith calls this "Faith according to the Closing Quotations." There can be little doubt what Bishop Lawrence's parishioners thought true stuff was.

Perhaps the dichotomy of the church and her values may be summed up by an Ivory Nativity Set (kept most of the year under lock and key). Here in glittering expense is captured the birth of the poor peasant Jesus — idols of immense value to suggest that earth's greatest possessions are not idols of immense value. The church would likely be the last to catch on to the inconsistency of an Ornate Nativity Set.

But Christmas always brings out the worst in the church. Church members who shop with mania in all of the expensive shops, gather in their holly-laden chapels to sing, "Away in a manger no crib for a bed," certainly glad that the poverty of Christianity's founder is not theirs. Buy, wrap, and give stuff, even to people you don't like very much so that all may remember that stuff is ultimate. Churches prone to teaching the non-validity of earthly treasure most of the year are willing each December to overlook the clock-radios and portable TV's nestled beneath the lush boughs of the evergreen tree.

Elton Trueblood has given us a possibly painful look at our double allegiance at Christmas:

> If·we are inclined to dispute the existence of materialism in the West, all that is required to convince us of its reality is a careful study of advertisements, particularly at Christmas. In preparation for the birthday of Him who had not where to lay His head, we are urged to buy for the wife a forty-thousand-dollar necklace or, for a couple, matching airplanes marked "His" and "Hers." [4]

No, Christmastide would not be a good time for the church to argue that she represents another set of values from those offered by the materialistic revolution.

The traditional church stands little chance of preaching her Doctrine of True Stuff and attracting any serious disciples with it. We must rather, somehow, recover our lost substance. Like St. Francis we need to forsake our affluence, for we cannot cling to it and convince anyone, ourselves notwithstanding, that we operate by Christ's values. For a long time a sumptuous Christianity has been claiming her values are different. Now she must find a way to demonstrate her stuff.

Establishing the substance of our intangible realities

will not be easy. In the current materialistic milieu we must pause amidst our greedy peers, standing guard over their stockpiles of things, and say, "These things are mine! Gaze on my invisible realities: redemption, eternity, peace of mind." In but a little time the thing-lovers around us will be able to tell how much we really esteem our possessions. Do we indeed cherish our substance, or would we trade it for a bigger pile of things if given the opportunity?

Further, those around us must see that our lives are not valuable to us for the exhilaration that comes from having. Let me explain. We have long heard the statement: "You can't take it with you!" By this we mean that things are of value only to the living. But to those for whom things are all-valuable, living is a necessity of itself. Dying is the end of the owner, and since owning is life's greatest station, death is life's greatest tragedy. Here is a demonstration of our intangible substance: death cannot be victorious to the committed materialist. It is a bleak disinheritance.

By contrast, let us examine the death of a contemporary missionary, the late Jim Elliot. At the time of his martyrdom, he was a man without material substance, at least very much of it. But he had amassed an impressive amount of ministry to human misery. A Wall Street tycoon might have been unimpressed if this missionary had said, "There are my holdings: an attempt in Christ's name, a dream energized by God's Holy Spirit, a love for my assassins." Yet when he died, there settled down on the world a strange aura of victory. He was indeed a man of wealth. His wife named her book on his life and death, *Through Gates of Splendor*. I remember the news release from my childhood, and what a thrilling challenge it brought to my adolescence. I well remember thinking, "Now he really had something." Like me, the whole world was impressed with his substance. For his commentary on the true stuff, he had written in his diary the ancient testimony of the martyrs:

He is no fool who gives what he cannot keep,
To gain what he cannot lose.

None of the thing-collectors can really challenge the true stuff.

But dying is not the only way you may demonstrate the true substance. It must be done in effective living. You will have to grant the materialists this: having does make them joyful. One has only to note the joy of a sweepstakes winner or a new inheritor to see the rapture of having. Now it is in this same logic that you as a believer in Christ demonstrates he actually has something. As this work contends, you really are a trustee of substance. Your joy should say to all that you are a person of great means.

St. Teresa called dour Christians "frowning saints." Frowning saints might say with leering conviction that Christ has given them much, but who indeed would want to risk asking for it? If you are a Christian who enjoys life and lives with a great deal of joy, you will make others envious of your inner holdings. Remember the robbers who fell upon St. Francis, took his clothes from him, and set him free? Imagine their surprise to hear him singing his way off into the snowy night.

It was hard to rob St. Francis. He didn't have the kind of wardrobe in which a self-respecting bandit would want to be arrested. He had no money. The bread tied at his belt was probably half eaten by birds, and he had not owned a horse since his days as a nobleman. All his assets were tied up in prayers, sermons, and kissing the untouchables. And while someone else always paid his fare at "prayer breakfasts," few men have left such a mark on history as he. Even the triple-crowned pope falls short of his burlap-clad brother. Still the demonstration of what he owned is his song in a drift of snow. As Charlie Brown so aptly put it: "Joy is the most infallible proof of the presence of God." Our argument is better sung than shouted.

Do you remember Paul and Silas in the Philippian jail (Acts 16:25)? After being beaten unmercifully and left in the agony of their scourging, they must have been tempted to survey skeptically their holdings. They had crossed into Greece with everything they owned either on their backs or packed into a carpet bag. And a Greek jail is as good a place as any for reflection. Could it have gone something like this?

PAUL: What have we got, Silas? We've preached our vocal cords loose in defense of the Gospel. Now what have we got?

SILAS: Not much, boss. A couple of K-rations and we're down to our last can of Sterno. My back is on fire.

PAUL: Mine, too! 'Course it's nothing like being crucified. You know it is really kind of an honor that He thought you and I were tough enough to send into Greece to tell these Europeans about the nature of true stuff.

SILAS: Yeah, Paul . . . Oh, my aching back! . . . you know, it's fantastic all the things we own in Christ. We're getting closer home every day . . .

PAUL: Think of that homecoming, Si . . . hey! Do you think you could manage one of our old Greek hymns? I hate to waste the acoustics of this place.

SILAS: Praise Christ! Let's sing up a storm or a quake!

And they sang at midnight. And when the jailer met them after the earthquake, he wanted to know where he could get in on their music.

Joy always makes more visible the invisible and more tangible the intangible. So when the thing-hoarders come to us and scrutinize our spirituality and say with contempt, "Have you nothing more than this?" we may say, "Stay longer, friend, and hear us singing in the snow."

# CHAPTER THREE

*God forbid that truth should be confined*
*to mathematical demonstration.*

WILLIAM BLAKE

# OF MIRACLES AND TECHNICS

Two plus two equals four. About that both Christians and technicians agree. Death plus Easter equals Life: this is another matter. Why? Many in our technocracy have sincerely added Easter and Death, and the sum is Zero. Those of us who know Christ have felt that the miraculous events on which our faith is based are as certain as the integers on the chalkboard of the calculus class. But the "natural" world believes in nothing substantial which cannot be formulated by some mathematical expression. Belief in biblical miracles has been largely displaced by a technical miracle — the computer. The cold capacitors and transistors of the electric brains have done their job mindlessly and obediently. Exempt from boredom, they have dealt with the most uninteresting integers: they have computed the margarine sales in Atlanta; they have predicted election results on the basis of precinct reports; they have with glassy gauges indicated the slightest deflection on Wall Street. They are the number-eaters: greedily ingesting decimals, binaries, and digits, and giving off deltas, quotients, products, sums, and milliequivalents. Somehow the computer seems to stand for the ideal toward which our increasingly technical society moves. Christian subjectivity, along with its fondness for the great miracles, has been abandoned in favor of something more measurable and mathematical. Lewis Mumford observed that in the mechanical realm, the human personality was an embarrassment to the new concept of "objectivity": to eliminate this "irrational" human factor was the common aim of both theoretic science and advanced technology. . . . From the eighteenth century on, the ideal of mechanical regularity and mechanical perfection entered into every human activity, from the observation of the heavens to the winding of clocks. . . . But now that the idea has been completely embodied, we can recognize that it had left no place for man. He is reduced to a standardized servo-mechanism: a left-over part from a more organic world. [1]

Thus there is a sense in which we modern men are in exile. Although we created the machines to serve us, now we have become their servants. We constructed our technological paradise, yet we were driven out of Eden because we lacked the formula to ourselves. We found that in trying to program our own personalities we could blow the tubes out of even the healthiest computer.

As man was a technic enigma, so was faith. Faith always involves a transcendence of natural law because it is built on the foundation of miracle. Miracles are those occurrences which inevitably catch the technologists with their logarithms down. There are no decent equations which explain the plague of frogs in Exodus or the transmutation of water into wine in John.

It isn't so much that the computer has rejected man and the miracles. It simply is not prepared to deal with them. This technical inadequacy of the machine would be all right with the faithful were it not for the sneering implication that there is really nothing which cannot be resolved into its component parts by the proper technicians. I will leave the substantial reality of man beyond the machine to Lewis Mumford or Charles A. Reich. But let us in this chapter consider

46

the reality of miracle and faith beyond the machine. Does miracle have substance? Is it really there? Before we go further, let us examine the importance of miracle in faith.

C. S. Lewis has stated the imperative relationship of miracle and faith:

> All the essentials of Hinduism would, I think, remain unimpaired if you subtracted the miraculous, and the same is almost true of Mohammedanism. But you cannot do that with Christianity. It is precisely the story of a great miracle. A naturalistic Christianity leaves out all that is specifically Christian. [2]

Let us never forget that standing at either end of the life of Christ is a great miracle: the virgin birth at the beginning and the resurrection at the end. The total package of miracles — His life, His birth, His resurrection — we refer to as the Incarnation. It is impossible to tamper with any aspect of Christ's incarnation without diminishing or destroying the faith. We will have surrendered the faith itself when we submit the miracles to the stamping mills.

It is strange indeed that technocrats in these latter days have become such a foe of the supernatural. In the beginning of the scientific era it was not so. Copernicus was a deeply religious man, as was Isaac Newton. Even Charles Darwin had studied theology. Johannes Kepler felt himself an ally of God and once boasted that God had to wait six thousand years for his first reader. Galileo observed that evidences of God's creativity caused him to worship the beauty of the Creator. Thus the rise of the technocracy slowly excluded the spiritual subjectivity which had been its original premise.

It is hard for us not to be overwhelmed by our creativity

and technology. Which of us have not stood before our toaster on a rainy Sunday morning and marveled at the ingenuity of technology? Thoreau marveled at the serenity of Walden. His more urban friend, Emerson, amazed by the blossoming technology of his day, remarked that his day excelled, "Outshining all recorded ages. In my lifetime, I have seen wrought five miracles, namely: 1. the steamboat; 2. the railroad; 3. the electric telegraph; 4. the application of the spectroscope to astronomy; 5. the photograph." Emerson's rapture seems naive; one wonders what he might have written had he been granted a view of a twentieth century child watching television in the back of his father's limousine on the way to the international airport.

We are not so awed as Emerson, although we may have more reason to be. But we simply cannot stand around gaping at every new marvel of our McLuhanesque age; we don't have the time for it. We have accepted technology, even when we have felt hostile toward it; after all, it was there and would not be shouted down. Everywhere there are machines. As H. L. Mencken has expressed, even the universe itself is part of man's mechanistic milieu:

> The cosmos is a gigantic flywheel making 10,000 revolutions a minute. Man is a sick fly taking a dizzy ride on it. [3]

Our day-in, day-out preoccupation with machines has led us to be predominantly mechanistic in all our presuppositions about God, who created order as well as miracles.

Eric Hoffer sees the machine age as man's way of vying with God. Hoffer suggests that when man was cast out of Eden, he got up, banged his fist on the closed gates, and said to the Creator, "I will return!"

Flinders Petrie, the Egyptologist, corroborates Hoffer in alleging, "The essential feeling of all the earliest work is rivalry with nature." The machine age has indeed become man's way of vying with God.

Technologically man has God "hands up" at the end of the barrel of his microscope. The Genesis creation narrative has been traded for a more rational and mechanistic evolution. Everywhere creation is seen as the mechanical ascent of elements. The opening line of the *Hellstrom Chronicle* runs: "The earth was not created with the gentleness of love; it was stabbed with the brutality of rape." This is the only view consistent to technocrats; everything must be mechanical. Only as cause struggles against senseless effect is the universe made.

The most intensely mechanical view of evolution has been presented by Pierre Teilhard de Chardin, the paleontologist who co-discovered Peking man. In our own day he has lent popular support to this view of mechanistic evolution. He has attempted to unite technology and evolution in a most unholy wedlock. The biblical Adam, in Teilhard's scheme of things, is replaced by the "phenomenon of man," who emerged from the natural machine on his evolutionary path to ultimate union with God. But this union with God is not the result of faith in the miraculous event, the Incarnation. Rather, it will come only with the acquisition of ultimate intelligence.

This union of God and Man redeems man by cosmic evolution. No longer is the world composed only of the lithosphere, hydrosphere, and atmosphere. Now, according to Teilhard, there is the "noosphere," a cerebral layer of consciousness forming with genuine continuity around the planet. Human mentality is the most worthy product of the evolutionary engine, and when it has reached its ultimate level of apprehension, it will merge with divine intelligence in the "noosphere." This point of the merger is designated the "omega point."

But the merger of the two minds is not a proposition of faith so much as it is a proposition of technology. The omega point is not reached by prayer or a trusting confidence in the miraculous. It is achieved by the complexification of the human intellect in higher and higher mathematical abstractions. As man draws nearer and nearer the omega point, he becomes increasingly depersonalized as a technicality of the machine. Teilhard in his scheme of things often refers to persons as universal "particles" and human minds as "granules."

Although Teilhard represents a radical departure from classic geology, classic theology, classic anthropology (and classic everything), he has been vastly influential. His view, accepted, not only eradicates the biblical view of salvation and destiny, it negates life as miraculous in itself. Spontaneity is not permitted in the predetermined program, and miracle is beyond question. Since Teilhard's God is impersonal, he cannot be really involved with persons in his world. Thus, with God comfortably out of the machine, man can take full credit for his natural supremacy. "After all," he reasons, "have I not climbed species by species to my present intelligence? Is not natural law the 'survival of the fittest'? Am I not the 'fittest'? Have I not by tooth and claw triumphed over the amoeba and amphioxus to stand on my present dais?"

Following this very reasoning, Desmond Morris was able to posit man seriously as the *Naked Ape*. In the primate's primitive struggle to survive, he became a hairless ape. All of his behavior and physique were created by causality. As a hunter ape, man ate his newly killed prey while it was yet warm by the temperature of blood: thus man still practices warming his food today. By these kinds of arguments Morris establishes man as "a happening" in the evolutionary engine.

From a purely mechanical viewpoint it is easy to understand how we in the technocracy have come to ourselves in a struggle with nature. It is easy to see how even Desmond Morris's view of man is more palatable to structured thought pattern than the Genesis view that the "LORD God formed man of the dust of the ground, and breathed into his nostrils the breath of life; and man became a living soul" (Gen. 2:7). The Bible's Adam is an embarrassing miracle to the machine, and therefore the machine cannot seriously entertain his divine creation as a possibility.

Technology may create but God may not. Aldous Huxley's *Brave New World* is a fictional extension of man's mechanistic vyings with God. In the "Central Hatchery and Conditioning Center," the glass-cased embryos are formed and developed and even conditioned before birth. The alpha babies are bred to exercise authority and control; the epsilon babies are bred to produce low intelligence, necessary to the faithful discharge of their meaningless roles in life. Life emanating from such formulated production is but a sterilized replica of biblical man.

By contrast the biblical Adam was a fresh and vital will, stretching in the ochre dust, walking with God in wonder. That Adam, who stirred to life in the new enchantment of the chirping forest, is not from the universal machine. Rather, he sprang from the divine image like a reflection on a clean mirror.

If we are the miracle of God, our ingratitude is blatant. It is cross impudence to proclaim ourselves the sculpture of the evolutionary machine. Isaiah's words have defined our presumption:

51

Is the potter of no more account than the clay?
Shall the thing that is made say of its maker,
  "He made me not";
Or the thing that is molded say of its molder,
  "He has no intelligence?"
                              (Isa. 29:16, *Smith-Goodspeed*)

Such may be the impudence of the technical machine. If
you have tended to view your origin as a mechanistic happening, you may be prone to view your continuance as a
function of the biotechnical machine. Medicine might
serve as the *locus classicus*. Medicine has developed chemi-
cals and tools to deal with most of the dread diseases. It
protects you. There are rules of thumb, basic even to
interns, and capable of extending your life where previously
it would have been lost. Research is steadily adding to this
technology. In the early days of medical research, great
lifesaving discoveries carried the awe of miracle about them.
Increasingly, however, you see them only as the logical
product of applied science.

Gone are the physicians who were miracle workers;
your doctor is a technologist. Coincidentally, many
physicians have increasingly viewed themselves as scientists, able to apply a specific body of knowledge to a
specific situation. Some (as opposed to the old family
doctor of yesteryear) feel they are more likely to do
their job well if they are not personally involved with
you as a patient; good science is best applied without emo-
tional interactions.

The beauty of the mystery of life has been blemished
by technical medicine. The organic physique is now
mostly utilitarian. Death may not be viewed as the
change of the living to the dead, but as a change of the
functioning organism to a usable salvage yard, whose
various parts may yet find use in the world of opera-
tion and supply. Corneas, kidneys, hearts are all usable,

provided they are in a state of reasonable repair; the cadaver itself can be used to teach the coming generation of scientists the functioning of the human machine.

Most of us are not opposed to the progress of medicine at all. But we are incensed by the growing apathy to life as a miracle and the tendency to view it as only the predictable motion of the biomachine. Is not life ravaged by technology when we come to view it so mechanically — when internal medicine is thought of in exactly the same way as an oil additive given to correct the carbon sludge in a gasoline engine? Have we not, by such very thought, equated miracle and technology?

We may be dangerously close to the end of the miraculous in medicine. Indeed, we possibly have already passed it. A passage from Malcolm Muggeridge may indicate that our total view of medicine is mechanized:

> The most ardent advocates of the heart transplants are prepared to admit that there will never be enough donors in the foreseeable future for the operation to be available for more than a minute proportion of those who might benefit from it. This is even taking into account all that the roads offer on a sunny weekend — a fruitful source of spare organs, as could be gathered from an aside when they were on the prowl for a donor in Groote Schuur Hospital in Cape Town. For the moment, it was said, no one suitable had shown up, but over the weekend they might have *better luck.* Properly organized, the roads should yield quite a harvest of serviceable spare parts, in flesh as well as metal. Nothing wasted on our motorways this weekend! [4]

When our view of medicine becomes this mechanical (if it is not already), life will no longer be seen as a miracle, but as a compatible technology. Perhaps that is the haunting meaning of a photograph of Philip Blaiberg holding his own heart in a glass beaker after his surgery in Cape Town. It was oddly like a mechanic holding a carburetor in a bath of kerosene.

To apply this kind of technology to the ministry of Jesus would impoverish the whole Christ Event. For the woman who had an issue of the blood, there would be sutures to secure the hemorrhage (Luke 8:43). For blind Bartimaeus there might be a cornea transplant (Mark 10:46). For Simon's fevered mother, aureomycin (Luke 4:38); for the deaf stammerer in Mark 7:32, a hearing aid and a therapist. Such a view implies, of course, that miracle is at best inconsequential and at least unsubstantial.

Now that we have seen the technical milieu in which miracle must find acceptance or pass away, we must move on to a search for its substance. Let us keep in mind that if we win no right for the existence of miracle, neither can we secure the existence of Christianity. The former is the breath and pulse of the latter. Let us, therefore, understand the importance of the question, "Does the miraculous have real substance?"

Only in the last couple of centuries have such questions even been permitted. From the time of the apostles onward, miracles were abundant in number, quality and acceptance. Did not Peter and John heal the lame man (Acts 3:2ff.)? Simon Magus (Acts 8:13) believed when he saw the wonders which Philip wrought. Paul also healed the father of Publius of a terrible fever (Acts 28:8). Throughout the Roman era and the Middle Ages, miracles were commonly reported, but as the world approached the machine age they became less and less frequent. And except for reports from American faith healers and the grotto at Lourdes, one rarely hears of miracles in these recent times.

You yourself may be taken in by this strange duplicity. You may be willing to accept the miracles as they are reported by the holy men of antiquity. But in the contemporary technocracy, they will not permit them standing room. You might, for instance, view with misty eyes Cecil B. DeMille's film, *The Ten Commandments*, wherein is the dividing of the Red Sea. But you cannot imagine it being done during the more recent Six-Day War, even by David Ben Gurion. You generally believe that Simon Peter walked on Galilee, but you would never believe he did it on Lake Erie, for example.

To explain this duplicity is probably quite easy. Your reverence for the Bible, venerated in time, causes you to accept it with little question. On the other hand, your subtle conditioning by technology causes you to be skep-accept it with little question. On the other hand, our subtle conditioning by technology causes us to be skeptical of any recent event that is alien to "good science."

One other observation is probably worth mentioning. Catholics apparently have the greatest capacity for accepting contemporary miracles. The exact reason for this is not clear, but it is probably that their well recorded traditions include the miracles of the saints down to the present times. Conversely, Protestants have largely ignored those traditions and mostly reverenced only biblical events.

A couple of practical illustrations will indicate the difference in Catholic and Protestant mystique toward revering miracles: the children in Fatima, Portugal, were visited successively by the Virgin as they tended their sheep. In honor of those visitations, a cathedral was erected. In a small Protestant church in North Carolina, some said that Jesus appeared on a Sunday morning during the 1960's. Nothing was built in that place except a general reputation for communal imagination.

If the Protestant mystique of doubt is the result of technical influence, it seems to me we are in the gravest danger of applying our mechanistic standards to biblical events. Any attempt to force them to measure up mathematically will destroy them.

In our frustration, we must cry out then, "Is there any way to prove that miracles really are substantial?" In a few cases the miracle is corroborated by the secular literature which parallels the era of the writing of the Scriptures. The only other "proof" which exists for biblical miracle lies in the examination of the influence of the event on the society of that day. Let us look first at those miraculous events which find some corroboration in history.

It may not be quite in keeping with the theme to start out by mentioning the flood saga of Genesis as a miracle, although certainly the salvation of Noah's family was considered such. It is interesting that the Babylonians produced a written saga, nearly identical in story to the Genesis narrative, called the Gilgamesh Epic (which antedates the writing of the Genesis account by centuries). Noah is called Utnapishtim, but the other incidentals of the story are nearly the same. The Greeks — in their counterpart of the Hebrew flood story — in the account of Decaulion and Phyrra charged them with repopulating the globe after the watery destruction of life. The existence of such parallel traditions should help point to the validity of the event. The instance of the biblical account might be further verified by an archaeological witness from Mount Ararat, the traditional landing site of the Ark. For a long time now, slivers of petrified wood have been found on the slopes of the mountain, and only recently a French archaeologist brought back from there an eighteen-inch, petrified board which showed evidences of being hand-planed.

Another example of historical parallels might be the destruction of Sennacherib's army (Isa. 37:36). This miracle occurs when the Jerusalemites are being threatened with a siege by the Assyrian Empire. The Prophet Isaiah publishes peace in the crisis, telling the king and the people not to be alarmed by the taunts of the huge Assyrian army outside their gates. Then, miraculously, God sends an angel through the camp of the Assyrians, and the army is decimated. Herodotus, the Greek historian, in mentioning the same event establishes its historicity. While Herodotus says the alien army was destroyed by the plague, the very mention of the event as history is an invaluable corroboration.

Miracle in the New Testament is harder to confirm by records contemporary to that time, with a single possible exception — the Star of Bethlehem. It is hardly reasonable that such an event would have been completely overlooked by all the rest of the world. There is one outstanding contemporary reference to the miraculous phenomenon by the Roman poet Virgil. Even Bultmann is agreed that Virgil's *Fourth Eclogue* may have been considered by Romans to be a prophecy of that Star. Although Virgil died in 19 B.C., his words are hauntingly reminiscent of Isaiah 11:6-9 as he describes the new utopian age:

> Now is come the last age of the Cumaean prophecy:
> The great cycle of periods is born anew,
> Now returns the maid, returns the reign of Saturn:
> Now from the high heaven a new generation comes down. . . .
> Untended shall the she-goats bring home their milk-swol'n udders,
> Nor shall the huge lions alarm the herds:
> Unbidden thy cradle shall break into wooing blossom.
> The snake too shall die, and die the treacherous poison plant;
> Assyrian spice shall grow all up and down. . . .

> Behold the world swaying her orbed mass,
> Lands and spaces of sea and depth of sky;
> Behold how all things rejoice in the age to come. [5]

According to Virgil's prophecy, Romans felt the new star ushered in the *Pax Augusti*; Luke opined that it ushered in the *Pax Christi*. But neither Virgil nor Luke would disagree about the reality of the celestial appearance.

The bulk of miracles does not have this sort of secular corroboration. Their validity is not so dramatically attested. The primary evidences for their authenticity must be found in the Bible itself. In examining the miracles, we must ask, "Does the narrative surrounding the accounts of the miracles seem a genuine reflection of their reality?" Or, on the other hand, do they appear to be magical attention-getters, inserted only to amaze the reader but wholly incidental to the narrative?

First of all, let it be firmly established that the whole account of the gospels is really a tale of the reaction to the teachings and miracles of Jesus. Even the story of His passion and crucifixion are the result of His teachings. But much of the gospel story is a reaction to His miracles. The early attempt to proclaim Him king comes as a result of His feeding the multitude (John 6); this seems the natural consequence to such a supernatural event. After his own resurrection, Lazarus becomes a biological curio to those who had attended his funeral (John 12:9). Again, the likelihood of that happening seems extremely probable and lends an atmosphere of credibility to the story.

The miracle of the virgin birth would seem utterly incredible considered alone. But the natural happenings in the narrative make it seem quite real. Mary may have left Nazareth to keep down the talk of the village busybodies (Luke 1:39). She marries Joseph only after his fears of Mary's infidelity have been allayed by an angel of the Lord (Matt. 1:18-25). Inspired by her estate as "highly favored among women" (Luke 1:42), she sings the *Magnificat*, whose captivating poetry would have been beyond a peasant girl such as herself." Some have said the virgin birth was a fabrication of the evangelists, who thought that including the event would serve as a slur on sex in behalf of the puritanical, primitive Christian ethic. But C. S. Lewis has answered the charge classically in saying that the virgin birth is no more a slur on the sexuality of the day than the feeding of the five thousand was a slur on the bakeries of that day. As with the other miracles, the circumstances which surround this one help to fix it as truth.

We must consider the Resurrection. After all, it is the central miracle of the Incarnation and one may not even be a Christian without believing it (Rom. 10:9). On this miracle stands the existence of the Christian faith (1 Cor. 15:1-26). Needless to say, it presents a supreme challenge to the technically oriented. Just as the virgin birth is an oblong enigma to the geneticist or obstetrician, so is the Resurrection to the anatomist or physiologist.

But apart from its nontechnical aspects, the miracle has a great deal to recommend it. After the death of Christ the mood of the gospels is most somber. Despair and gloom are oppressive. Then the apostles are rallied back into a preaching and witnessing unity, characterized by great joy. What else could have accomplished this besides the Resurrection? Further, there is a kind of numbness in the closing chapters of the gospels, caused by a compulsion to believe the fantastic, along with a reluctance to do so. The women babble the exciting news to the disciples, but — alas! — their report seems as "idle tales, and they believed them not" (Luke

24:11). Then, after they finally do come to believe, the disciples try to tell the news to Thomas, who, stricken by their naïveté, affirms in dogmatic skepticism: "Except I shall see in his hands the print of the nails, and put my finger into the print of the nails, . . . I will not believe" (John 20:25).

Besides this numbness there is a kind of edgy expectancy. With Christ always showing up mysteriously behind sealed doors (John 20:26) or appearing silently and unannounced on desert roadways (Luke 24:13ff.) or standing pensively wrapped in the gray mist of morning on a Galilean beach (John 21:4), they never know quite where they will meet Him. This kind of uneasiness about having a "dead" Messiah unpredictably among them is further evidence from the Scripture itself of the reality of the Resurrection.

Perhaps Peter Marshall's great logic should stand last in the chapter. Remember that, according to tradition, all the apostles except one were martyred. The late Scottish preacher argued that only the truth of the Resurrection would have caused them to pay for the Christian faith with their blood. For while it might be supposed that they fabricated the story of Easter, it is unlikely they would have died for an imaginative falsehood. The Resurrection was the great, irrefutable truth that forged the apostles into a band of martyrs. Their martyrdom is witness to that chiefest of all the miracles.

Therefore, when we are hailed before any technical tribunal and asked for the evidence of our miraculous trust, we are not utterly impoverished. For while we can offer them no photograph of Jesus walking out of the tomb, we can extend to them the natural milieu which surrounds the miracles. We can say to them that just as morality is real, so are the miracles, although both of them are beyond objectification and measurement. And for those who have experienced the new birth — itself a miracle — the argument is answered by human meaning. But since meaning is the consideration of a later chapter, we must stop here.

Amos Wells spoke well of the substance of miracle when he wrote of the man with the withered hand (Luke 6:10), whom Christ restored:

> Praise God! Praise God! Give me my tools again!
> I am a man again, a man for work.
>
> . . . no more a bandaged cumberer.
> And did you hear them muttering at him?
> And did you see them looking sour at me?
> They'll cast me from the synagogue, perchance:
> But let them: I've a hand, a hand, a hand!
> And, ah . . . to think He goes about
> So quietly, and does such things as this,
> Making poor half men whole. . . . [6]

This is Christ's greatest miracle — the renovation of the race with joy and soul. And no empiricist may deny to us the firmness of our substance.

# CHAPTER FOUR

Doubt my sanity but acknowledge my immortality.

WILLIAM LLOYD GARRISON
from *The Dissenter*

# AGAINST ABSURDITY

MEANINGLESSNESS may be the eminent neurosis of our times. William March's *Unknown Soldier*, wounded and wallowing in the barbed wire, was put to death by a kind German officer. As the soldier's eyes fluttered closed, he said, "I have broken the chain. . . . I have defeated the inherent stupidity of life." Death increasingly is viewed, not as a triumph over circumstance, but as the end of the empty routine. It is triumphant only in the sense that it dissolves cyclical nothingness.

It seems most unnatural that our culture, basking in affluence, should be ridden with despair. Less prosperous times have yielded far more hope. It seems to be established that the eras of flagrant materialism are times of greatest pessimism. Times of want and oppression, on the other hand, have produced the poetry of optimism: the Negro slaves sing their joyous spirituals with the lash scars gleaming in ebony; but with far more substance in these latter days, their songs are of oppression. Similarly, Christianity under the persecution of the Caesars burned with zeal and apocalyptic optimism; in this, the day of its opportunity, it proclaims God is dead. It is the Jews of the Exile who dream, not Solomon's obese courtiers. Thus, heavy with possessions, we Space Agers whimper ourselves to sleep in our gilded dwellings.

Our war against meaninglessness has uncovered a cache of quaint weapons for the struggle. We slash at senselessness with bourbons on the rocks, amphetamines, and sexual promiscuity. We buy psychotherapy. We contemplate the beautiful mysticism of the East. We titillate our fascination with cabalism. We bare our souls in sensitivity therapy. We fight our emptiness with giddy laughter which is too nervous to be the authentic mock-up of joy that we would like it to appear. We cry.

In the desperation of the search, many try Christianity. For many, even that quest is barren. The church, which should be producing truth and meaning, produces only the lubricant which makes its own machinery go. And those who hunger for the substance of existence are only offered a committee presidency, and so they do not stay for church. And the statisticians coldly observe that the rate of church growth is barely keeping up with the incidence of suicide.

Thus comes that haunting question. Christians must either answer it or be prepared to accept forever their own irrelevancy: "Does Christianity contain substantial meaning?" The world wants the question answered, not with an "amen," but with a demonstration. No one is crying out for the theory of our creeds and sermons; the cry is for authentication of our claim to meaning.

Men have asked with dread, "Is there anyone home in the universe?" They posed the question after they had heard our finest choral arrangements of the *Creation*. People were prone to believe that we held the key to meaning — until they caught us quarreling on the way home from church and sat beside us in the psychiatrist's waiting room. Their despair tore them even deeper when they heard us emerging from our noisy "solemn assemblies" and piously asking, "Anyone for sky pie?"

We know generally "how" we should live. We are trying to discover "why." Nietzsche reminds us that "He who has a *why* to live can bear with almost any *how*." The hunger for the "why" is burning its way through the current age. The pathetic social state is pictured by the seekers living in a mechanized wilderness and singing of the coming of the Age of Aquarius, the Water Bearer. The thirst for meaning is intense.

Viktor Frankl is a psychiatrist worth listening to. The famed leader of the Third Viennese School of Psychotherapy (the previous two were headed by Freud and Adler), he emerged from the horrors of the Auschwitz death camp determined to deal with the "why" of existence. Seeing life stripped to stark minimum forged his philosophy. Men under those rigorous deprivations abandoned all interest in sex — contrary to the Freudian belief. Life *in extremis* did not pursue the course of power — the preoccupation of Adlerian thought. Only one thing transcended the ugliness of human reduction: hope. Meaning lived in the gaunt and silent inmates of Auschwitz.

Frankl alludes to a survey taken in France in which 89 percent of the people polled admitted that everyone needs something for which to live. Also, 61 percent of those interviewed said there was someone or some issue for which they were willing to die. [1] Jean-Baptiste Clamence, in Albert Camus's *The Fall*, did not rate God very high as the kind of meaning for which one would die:

> Ah, *mon cher*, for anyone who is alone, without God and without a master, the weight of days is dreadful. Hence one must choose a master, God

being out of style. Besides, that word has lost its
meaning. . . .[2]

The entire Christian faith rests upon the antithesis to
Camus. Its very continuance depends upon that antithesis. God is entire meaning. And Paul's profound
reduction of all Christian meaning appears in the statement: "For to me to live is Christ" (Phil. 1:21).

While Frankl (being Jewish) would not say that all
ultimate meaning is Christian, he does say it is spiritual:

> The appropriate and adequate therapy is not
> psycho-therapy (mind therapy) in general but
> rather logotherapy (meaning therapy); a thera-
> py, that is, that dares to enter the spiritual di-
> mension of human existence. (parentheses mine)[3]

Interpreting this statement in a Christian context is
our only hope of confronting absurdity redemptively in
this present age. Only by action bound in compassion
may we hope to demonstrate that we have a "why" to
the question of life.

It is doubtful that even the most rigid determinists
do not from time to time wish to deny their own dogma
and discover meaning. Even those who view the universe as a self-driven machine that permits no abstractions will from time to time reach for love or offer a
prayer comfortably beyond earshot of their unbelieving
peers. The Marquis de Sade could argue convincingly
that everything was chemically determined, even morality; therefore, any happenstance was right and just. But
during his confinement in Charenton he complained
about his "unjust" treatment by the jailers. He spent
hours pouting over his wife's letters although, according
to his own argument, they were just the chemical and
vascular etchings of his autonomous universe. Is it possible that de Sade himself was reaching for the "why"?

Existentialism (secular), with all of its various facets, has been brutally destructive in its assault on human meaning. Jean-Paul Sartre and Albert Camus, the French existentialists, say that while life is entirely absurd, the exercise of human will is self-authenticating. Even charitable acts have no moral and spiritual content but, in deciding to be moral or charitable, one becomes real in an illusionary world. Sartre's play No Exit is a picture of man locked in an absurd universe and, while living must go on, it goes on pointlessly. Since Camus, as well as Sartre, has produced a great deal of fiction, his views have also been widely read by the populace.

Jaspers, the Swiss existentialist, speaks of authenticity coming only through what he calls the "final experience." This is any experience of such an impressive nature that it gives one the assurance he is really there. Without that experience every existence is undemonstrable, being buried in bleak meaninglessness.

All the realm of contemporary literature, including screenplays, has been used to echo the theme of contemporary existentialism. Since it would be foolhardy even to attempt to deal with the examples in this short a work, we will not give specific consideration. Let a single quote stand for the whole:

> There are always too many rotten pillars left standing, too much festering humanity for man to bloom. The superstructure is a lie and the foundation is a huge, quaking fear. . . . Who that has a desperate, hungry eye can have the slightest regard for these existing governments, laws, codes, principles, ideals, ideas, totems and taboos? Out of nothingness arises the sign of infinity; beneath the everlasting spirals slowly sinks the gaping hole. . . . I see that behind the nobility of [man's] gestures there lurks the spectre of the ridiculousness of it all. . . . he is not only sublime but absurd. [4]

Just as the doctrine of the absurd has been advanced on the literary front, so it has been advanced by modern artists, especially the surrealists and the Dada school. Life is essentially meaningless. One of the poems of Dadaist Kurt Schwitters contains this verse:

> Bumm bimbimm bamm bimbimm
> Bumm bimbimm bamm bimbimm
> Bumm bimbimm bamm bimbimm
> Bumm bimbimm bamm bimbimm [5]

The rest of the poem is this same kind of jumbled syllables.

In the current music and drama, the absurd is set forth in an increasing number of ways. The disillusioned and hopeful have turned their faces toward Christians and asked where is the substance of meaning. The skeptic's escape from the theater of the absurd is impossible, yet there is a sense in which God may actually be stalking us with dread to offer us meaning in the Person of His Son.

Arthur Gossip relates that in the Hebrides you can never get away from the sea. It is impossible to try. No matter where you go in the islands, the green tides thrust an inland arm at you and constantly remind you that you are on an island. Nor can you there forget your predicament, for at some unexpectant jetty it swings at you with a sudden inlet or thrusts some rocky cove into your awareness. Thus, like Francis Thompson's *Hound of Heaven*, He follows us through the existential deserts, extending the overflowing cup with refreshing love.

The source of Christian meaning resides in two concepts — the Person and the Book. Although each of these sources is an entity in itself, they are interdependent and may not be separated. All that we know of the Person is recorded in the Book, and the whole reason for the Book is to direct men to the Person. Most of those people beyond meaning have discovered neither the Person nor the Book.

The Christian community ought to ache for those who have achieved academic excellence in the arts and sciences but are fettered to absurdity. Perhaps the acme of compassion for Christian intellectuals would be prayerful concern for the atomic physicist who can smash an atom but does not know the music of the Psalms or the harsh prose of the passion passages. One wonders if the Dada artist or the Heidegger disciple has ever been told about Christ by the Christian who walks the campus under the compulsion of sheer love. One thing is certain: these are days of opportunity for the courageous witness. The hunger for meaning in these times is everywhere evoking a curiosity about both the Person and the Book. Still, many academicians are suspicious of anything which transcends the mechanical cybernetics of our computerized living. So meaning is left standing in the wings, while the characters busy themselves in the theater of the absurd.

Two other factors are often involved in the absurdists' rejection of the faith proposition. First, there is the sadism of the atheist intellectual. While this is not always true, still with predictable frequency the atheist intellectual has exhibited a kind of glee in publishing absurdity. A case in point is the professor of philosophy who loves intimidating college freshmen with the absurd. With the fiendish inner satisfaction of the Grand Inquisitor, he explodes his familiarity with *Being and Nothingness* all over his church-trained underlings. He so enjoys mutilating adolescent mentality with his *angst*-bombs that his own conversion to Meaning would be less probable than the late Adolph Eichmann embracing Judaism.

71

Often the absurdists who are not sadists are maso-
chists. These love persecuting themselves. They get a
delicious feeling of atonement by staring at the Medusa
of existence. They love the black vacuity of the pit.
Sobbing in their sleep without hope is a negative in-
trigue they could never abandon. They are preoccupied
with despair and find it a compelling pastime. Especially
is this true if they are creative writers or painters. Cap-
turing "nothingness" on canvas or typewriter paper may
lead them ultimately to Jaspers' "final experience." And
those who do it well enough discover that their absurdity
is marketable in galleries and newsstands; perhaps these
could not afford to embrace Meaning.

From the very outset those who wish to probe the
Book for meaning must fix one point clearly. Just as
logic is related to knowledge, so mystery is related to
faith. The entire success of the Meaning venture depends upon this. Those who seek to make the Book
match the induction of their chemistry text will arrive
nowhere in their search. Mystery is the *sine qua non*
of Christian meaning.

In *Brothers Karamazov*, the illegitimate Smerdyakov
is being introduced to the Bible by Old Gregory, his
pious foster father. The old man begins the reading with
Genesis and the creation account. But Smerdyakov re-
fuses to believe the Bible story because of what seems
an inconsistency: whereas light was created on the first
day, the sun is not created until the fourth day. Since
Smerdyakov reasons that light comes from the sun, he
loses confidence in the whole scriptural account. Immediately following his attempt to harmonize that inconsistency, he is taken with his first epileptic seizure,
a disease that is to follow him the rest of his life.

Any person who, like Smerdyakov, tries to force logic
into his view of the Scriptures is destined to end up in

jangling intellectual epilepsy. Salvation is God's conclusion to meaningless living and dying. God offers us the beautiful gift without all the explanation and procedural data. Knowing the great "why" of life, we are to trust Him with the "how" mechanics.

But the Stainless Steel Technocracy cannot easily endure mystery. There are millions of Christians who themselves are not content to live with unsolved mystery. So they live in seething despair that their redemption, while meaningful, is hidden from them. The very answers they seek place them on a course of "automatic destruct." The answers they seek would not enhance their security — they would destroy it.

Faith and mystery are codependent. Eliminate either one and you have destroyed the other. Faith cannot be faith once it is fully explained and the mystery is gone. Remember the maxim: "Great truths are like butterflies — you kill them when you pin them down." God can always act at vectors and angles that will not comfortably nestle into human gray matter. Suppose for a moment that the mystery-prober were able to solve all the mysteries. Would he lord it over all the rest of us who had not managed his science? Would he not be prone to boast, "Come, see my little God and the tables that chart His thoughts"?

Still the *mysterium* of faith, once accepted, does solve some things. The Christ-student cannot prove the existence of God by logistics, but he can avoid the unwieldy dynamics of proving there is not one. Atheists and agnostics who live in the vacuum of the absurd often forget there are at least as many unanswerable items in their philosophies as there are in the Christian faith. Which is it easier to answer: the mystery of the Trinity or the origin of the universe without a God?

This might be illustrated by the meeting of the atheist

(earlier generations called him an infidel) Robert Ingersoll and the great Congregational pastor Henry Ward Beecher. Ingersoll was renowned for his militant atheism and his cutting debates with the pious, where he nearly always managed to "prove" there was no God. His meeting with Beecher occurred in the pastor's study in Plymouth Church in Boston. Part of the decor of the study was a beautifully made celestial globe, an attractive piece of art, meticulously constructed. Ingersoll scrutinized it and said, "Henry, that's magnificent! Who made it?" The pastor answered with sparkling wit, "Why, Robert, nobody made it, it just happened."

In the illustration Ingersoll and Beecher represent two poles, faith and antifaith. Some, like Ingersoll, tend to be know-it-all in attitude toward believers. But they cannot answer a good many questions satisfactorily — questions about personality, psyche, guilt; for such, the universe itself is there but present without meaning.

Perhaps the major difference between the Christian and the skeptic is this: the Christian accepts the mysterious God, and the universe is solved. The atheist denies God and must therefore live in a mysterious universe.

The meaning available in the Book is sealed off because of our unwillingness to embrace mystery. To a degree this is also true of the meaning of the Person. Christ is also mysterious. His miraculous incarnation is inaccessible to those who take in truth only by mental osmosis.

But perhaps the greatest barrier to the skeptic's salvation is the lack of confrontation. We have kept the Christ in the crypt. For some unexplainable reason the world is suspicious of all mention of God out of the proper gothic context. In fact, it is clear that any reference to God in the secular realm seems intrusive.

Thus Jesus, like a medieval Bible, has seemed chained to the church. The church-jailed Christ is utterly incomprehensible when set alongside Jesus' Great Commission: "Into all the world" — into the barber shops, boutiques, restaurants, bookstores, markets, arenas.

Yet when you as a witness dare to utter the name of Christ in the area of your involvements, you will be told in one way or another, "Shh, there is a time and a place for that. The time is eleven o'clock on Sunday morning. The place is the stained glass forum of antiquities, otherwise called the church."

St. Peter on his way into the temple passed a cripple at the gate. In compassion and, more important, in the sunlight and fresh air of the outside world, he said to the man, "In the name of Jesus!" In our own day the cripple might have said, "Please, not here . . . I mean . . . look, everyone is staring. I would rather you take care of this next time I come to church. I'll tell you what — I'll meet you Easter in the vestibule." Having said that, he would sell Peter a bumper sticker reading, "Hire the Handicapped."

What happened, to the contrary, was a thing of beauty. The man walked, even leaped. It all happened because the name of Jesus was spoken to a Hebrew etching, attached immobile to an unyielding gate. Then the etching lived with animation and verve. He flung his bag of pencils in the ecstasy of his wholeness and ran.

To run is a simple act. He ran because it seemed the thing to do when he had never before done it. He ran because Jesus said to him excitedly, "Run, child! let them know that there is power in My name to bring madness into the market. Run if you love God! Let them doubt that your mind may have strength, but not your ankles, run! RUN! RUN!"

75

How desperately the church needs to learn that there is power in the name of Jesus spoken in the sunlight. It leads to adventure and meaning. That name might still set the dumb to singing and cripples to sprinting athletically with a supple coordination through a host of cynics, if we Christians would say it in the warm sunlight, witnessing in every place.

Jesus lived free in the world of the Caesars, striding through it with power and dignity and authority and healing and meaning. Only in these latter times have we captured Him and subdued Him and forced Him to live in the dark and preside over our solemn and candle-lit assemblies. Like a captured animal, the institutional Christ roars against our euphonies. Pacing nervously, He longs to escape the church house and meet the needs of the suffering and the damned beyond.

Thus we are called to participate in this ministry of meaning. He has sent us to go boldly and preach optimism. And the impact of the truth we share will be for some a release from captivity. In a brilliant flash of insight some will have that "final experience" in which all their living will be authenticated.

When Helen Keller was telling her life story, she recorded what she called a "detonation." One day her teacher placed in her hand the key that was to unlock her silent blackness. Never hearing or seeing, she had no way to learn sign language or to communicate with signs or symbols. She had been touching hundreds of objects but there was no way to know what they were without sight and sound. In her own language she wrote of her experience with her teacher:

> She brought me my hat and I knew I was going out
> into the warm sunshine. This thought, if a wordless
> sensation can be called a thought, made me hop

and skip with pleasure. We walked down the path to the well-house, attracted by the fragrance of honeysuckle with which it was covered. Someone was drawing water and my teacher placed my hands under the spout. As the cool stream gushed over my hand she spelled into the other the word *water*, first slowly, then rapidly. I stood still, my whole attention fixed upon the motion of her fingers. Suddenly, I felt a misty consciousness as of something forgotten — a thrill of returning thought; and somehow the mystery of language was revealed to me. I knew that w-a-t-e-r meant that wonderful, cool something that was flowing over my hand. That living word awakened my soul, gave it light, hope, joy, set it free! There were barriers still, it is true, but barriers that in time could be swept away.

I left the well-house eager to learn. Everything had a name, and each name gave birth to a new thought. As we returned to the house, every object that I touched seemed to quiver with life. That was because I saw everything with the strange, new sight that had come to me. [6]

Young Helen might have appeared strange to any who saw her with her new ecstasy, but she was athrill with "detonation." A silent, dumb, absurd world was exploding with singing life, and she was in the middle of it all.

My detonation was Christ. He has been the detonation for many lives. In fact, my testimony of Him would be Helen Keller's words: "That living Word awakened my soul, gave it light, hope, joy, set it free!" The world for me is new every morning, because of Him who makes all things new.

I had lived in my plain world long enough before the detonation came. Now the universe swells with His glory. Since He is Lord, the very "heavens declare the

glory of God" (Ps. 19:1). I love Him just as I discovered Him — vast but personal, near but mysterious,
offering men everything but His own ultimate self-dis-
closure. Living itself has become believing this unbe-
lievable Christ (Phil. 1:21).

ENTER: meaning
EXIT: absurdity

# CHAPTER FIVE

*No excellent soul is ever exempt from a mixture
of madness.*

ARISTOTLE

# PROFILE FOR MADNESS

CHRISTIANITY is a strange faith indeed. It is the very bread of life to those who own it and a most quaint and idiotic affliction to those who pass it by. To those who have summed up the tenets of faith and unbelief and opted in favor of skepticism, the pious man may seem a madman. In fact, the Christian may appear to have a posture for insanity which feeds on such strange teachings as trinitarianism and resurrection. The hostility of the snobbish skeptic may focus on the Bible, which he views as the infernal source of all Christian madness. It is his feeling that the whole of Christendom might be cured by psychotherapy and secularism were it not for the Scriptures taught and reverenced in those gothic asylums called churches.

Sooner or later every believer meets the challenge of the "Sane." The Sane are those who, having examined Christianity clinically, have decided that faith is somehow beneath their rational dignity. As alluded to already, for some reason they are prone to be evangelistic. They preach the sanity of skepticism as salvation from scriptural madness.

This chapter purposes to help the believer over his defensiveness. To any skeptic convinced of our madness it does little good to protest our sanity anyway. It is probably better to concur with the diagnosis of the Sane than to risk ensnaring ourselves by protesting the accusation with fiery and glandular debate, which might only confirm his charges.

So let us accept our profile for madness. Let us make it clear, however, that it is not the same kind of mental splintering that Nietzsche (who by the way was one of the Sane) endured the last eleven years of his life. Nor is it the same kind of wild disorientation that the Marquis de Sade experienced at the Charenton Lunatick Asylum (he being another of the Sane). Ours, rather, is a happy madness given that label by others. It must be said, too, of our madness what Polonius said of the demented Prince Hamlet: "Though this be madness, yet there is method in it."

The profile for madness is a tradition as old as Christianity itself. Jesus, our Prince and Founder, faced many of the same charges against sanity that His followers face. On one occasion the Sane of Century One said of Him, "He hath Beelzebub!" (Mark 3:22). This was their way of saying to Him, "You are mad!" In pre-Freudian history (which most of history has been), to accuse any man of "demon possession" was the equivalent of calling him "schizo" in our time. Thus, to call a man "possessed of Beelzebub," the king of demons, was to make the most pointed accusation against his sanity.

If they accused Jesus and — as we shall discover in this chapter — many others of mixed mentality, how shall we escape their slurs? But when the accusation comes, the believer is to meet it without retaliation. Is it not all right if we are called what He was called? Remember: "The servant is not greater than his lord; neither he that is sent greater than he that sent him" (John 13:16).

We need to remember also that Jesus once said, "Woe unto you, when all men shall speak well of you!"

82

(Luke 6:26). Perhaps this statement may be used as a reliable guide to the seriousness of Christian devotion. When a believer crosses the threshold of faith, his reputation may become controversial. Some will admire the crossing. But some will feel that his convictions are too extreme, his habits too "churchy," his devotion overdone.

Admittedly my experience is small, but I have known few dedicated Christians for whom there did not exist a great deal of criticism. And generally the more serious the commitment, the more vehement the criticism.

James Thurber told of a lanky, prophetic-looking man who was always disheveled but went around Thurber's boyhood hometown crying through a megaphone, "Get ready! Get ready! The world is coming to an end!" Around the neighborhood he was affectionately known as the "get-ready" man. Being a Thurber admirer, I much like that story. But perhaps it illustrates the inconsistency of our time. For whatever his appearance might have been, the "get-ready" man was right! The world is coming to an end. So, at least, his prophecy is dependable.

To be sure, the "get-ready" man may have gone about it all wrong; but the story reflects the tongue-in-cheek attitude which the Sane of our generation have regarding the committed. To them, we have a madness only moderately different from that of Mr. Get Ready. One cannot help but wonder how Thurber would have reacted to John the Baptist.

Now if there was ever a "get-ready" man, John was it. He was a little unkempt in his camel's hair and leathern girdle; he may have looked as though he had just swung in out of the veldt. Still, he said, with embarrassing volume, "Get ready, for the kingdom of God is at hand." Doubtless, some thought he overpreached. Certainly the queen thought so, as she did not appreciate

83

the wild man meddling in her sophisticated sexual intrigues with her brother-in-law. But Jesus said of God's "get-ready" man, "Among them that are born of women there hath not risen a greater than John the Baptist" (Matt. 11:11). But in the same passage (Matt. 11:18) He reminded them that everyone said John the Baptist was possessed of devils, hence mad.

Perhaps it is poor taste to compare Thurber's and Matthew's "get-ready" men, for the only thing similar about them was their general reputation. But if this is the general reputation of John the Baptist, may we possibly hope that our commitment to Christ can end in anything less serious? In this Space Age, real faith often appears more insane for the fact that God Himself seems old and out of things. J. B. Phillips tells of a psychological test recently given to a group of students in their older teens. They were asked, "Do you think God understands radar?" Almost all the students said with laughter, "No!" Thus they demonstrated that God was out of the secular machine and therefore not relevant to this age.

This has compounded the problem: God to the swingers is a white-haired, flowing-robed something off the ceiling of the Sistine Chapel and completely unnecessary. Therefore the new disciples must appear piqued by His irrelevancies.

Neither books nor movies have helped to establish the sanity of the committed. Frequently the cinema industry has been most unkind in characterizing, even stereotyping, those who believe. This has been particularly true of evangelicals.

The Catholics, due to better lobbying and committee control, have managed to make themselves look better. Let's examine some for instances: *The Shoes of the Fisherman* creates a generally positive impression of the pope, Kiril Lakota. *The Sound of Music* left enrapt audiences in love with the laughable, lovable sisters of Salzburg. Then there was that wonderful wedding of dedication and aviation, Sister Patrill, the Flying Nun. The etceteras in this amiable Catholic front are endless.

Now let us contrast this with the light in which evangelicals are presented. For instances: there is the *Elmer Gantry* bias which comes through in many movies, in which the evangelical resembles at best a hypocrite and at worst a nincompoop. There is Somerset Maugham's "Rain," where the Protestant missionary manages to seduce one of his converts. Usually evangelical worshipers are shown going to church in patched overalls and singing, "Rock o'Hages, cliff fur me," with stunning nasality. Naturally, in such scenes the evangelical tradition appears not only subintelligent but definitely Dogpatch.

This is too often the picture, unpleasant but realistic. I have drawn it only because it ought to be understood that it is rarely possible, especially in evangelical Christianity, to serve God and one's own reputation at the same time. If someone's sense of security depends on having "all men speak well" of him, he can never be secure in following Christ. Further, the Acts 3 record of the early Christians makes it clear that not all the charges of madness brought by the Sane are worded in some frontal attack. For instance, on the day of Pentecost Peter and his friends were filled with the ecstasy of the Spirit of God.

(Perhaps we need to say at this point that we madmen are never quite responsible for our actions at a moment when we are filled with the Holy Spirit. We are radically happy and ultra-enthusiastic and so emotionally elevated that we may go a bit overboard in our felicity. In these moments we do not appear dangerous, only

85

humorous. At such times the Sane are not afraid of our madness, only entertained by it. So most were amazed at Peter's joy syndrome that day.)

Being more amused than frightened, the Sane at Pentecost joshed each other, elbow to rib cage, and said of this droll kind of epilepsy, "I say they're a jolly lot, these Christians, full of new wine as they are." Well, everyone was having a good time: the Christians were giddy with the Spirit: the Sane were giddy with the side show. Perhaps even Peter was laughing with a low rumble when he got up and said, "I know what you're thinking, but it isn't wine; not even Christians get drunk at nine in the morning" (cf. Acts 2:15). Their joyful madness, however, did resemble that utter bliss that fades into a super hangover more than it resembled any serious affliction of mind.

Things were different back in those days when Christians still drank a little. Now, in our abolitionist teetotalism, our madness is seldom confused with drunkenness. Now, for our more unreasonable doctrines, they say the same thing of us: "You are mad!"

(For once, perhaps, I should like to be called drunk rather than mad. But, since I am one of those teetotalers who takes not even a "little wine for his stomach's sake" [translation: Pepto Bismol], the Sane will never say of me that my problem is the taste of new wine.)

The Apostle Paul may be partly to blame for the unfortunate state of our milieu. He was a theologian. In this sense he was different from Peter, an evangelist. Evangelists can see the humor in everything and sometimes fill their revivalism with loads of jokes and happy hymns. So their madness at least seems a happy addiction.

Theologians, on the other hand, appear to have the worst kind of madness. They meditate in gray cells and tear themselves over "neo-anythings" that seem a threat to the "faith . . . once delivered unto the saints" (Jude 3). They seem multi-ulcered and distracted by a constant need to rave about the great teachings or some threat to them. Thus their mental state appears infinitely more serious than does the evangelists'.

The point may be best understood by seeing Paul of Tarsus as he stands before King Agrippa defending the Resurrection. Festus, the Roman who listened to the sermon, said at its conclusion: "You are beside yourself; much learning has made you mad!" Paul protested by saying in response, "I have not been driven mad; I am sane" (from Acts 26:24, 25). But alas, his protest was unconvincing and Festus went unconverted. The difference between Paul and Peter may point to one other fact: people would rather listen to a happy drunk than to a seriously afflicted madman. Paul had earlier experienced the same accusation on Mars Hill (Acts 17: 32) when the Athenians made fun of his obsession with the Resurrection. Thus Paul had learned to accept his profile for madness. There are several indications that group opinion had chipped Paul's confidence in his sound mentality, and he pleaded, "Let no man think me a fool" (2 Cor. 11:16). Or again, "I speak as a fool" (2 Cor. 11:23). Once indignantly he said, "I shall not be a fool" (2 Cor. 12:6). Not only was Paul aware that his convictions often made him appear a fool, but also he knew that, to the Sane, the entire Christian faith appeared a bulky slice of insanity, in contrast with the orderly and commonly held Olympian religions.

Paul said, "the preaching of the cross is to them that perish foolishness" (1 Cor. 1:18). In reference to the general insinuation about Christianity he said, "It pleased God by the foolishness of preaching to save them that believe" (1 Cor. 1:21). From these and even more passages that we might examine, we may conclude that Paul was aware of his reputation and the reputation of the faith.

The apostle did have one other significant thing to say about "Christian madness." He said it in reference to "speaking in the unknown tongue" or in spiritual "ecstasy" (as a later translation of the Bible has it). There were those, Paul felt, who were *needlessly* fostering the impression that Christians were mad. They were doing this by a showy and incoherent worship service in which they got a little carried away with their emotions and babbled in the "unknown tongue." Paul thought their conduct was reprehensible, making the condemnation of the Sane look reasonable. He reminded the Corinthians that you can make more converts by a spoonful of order than you can by a barrel of glossalalia. He put it to them rather bluntly: "If therefore the whole church become together into one place, and all speak with tongues, and there come in those that are unlearned, or unbelievers, will they not say that YE ARE MAD?" (1 Cor. 14:23, emphasis added).

Paul had pointed up an interesting issue. Doubtless, any Christian who takes seriously his own commitment to Christ will, from time to time, be called a fool of some sort. If he is not compliant in his loyalty to Christ, he will frequently receive that "Come-with-me-to-Menninger's" look. But why deliberately indulge in practices which alienate the Sane and needlessly put relatively "pious" people in the "looney" group?

So it is clear that some kinds of "madness" have more respectability than others. An insanity that loves Christ but does not talk in tongues is a more palatable madness than its opposite. The denomination to which I belong is a "winner" with many because it offers a more moderate madness. Its coefficient-of-catalepsy index is just halfway between the Pentecostals and the Episcopalians. Your madness would be unacceptable in my church if you should suddenly rise in a service and begin to talk in the "unknown tongue." Too, footwashing would be questioned even if one supplied his own basin. On the other hand, the madness would appear equally acute for anyone who wanted to discuss seriously C. S. Lewis or Apostolic Succession. He would seem immediately cankered who genuflected at the communion table.

Still, I love the particular kind of madness my denomination teaches. Like most in my church, I feel very secure about halfway between Billy Sunday and the Archbishop of Canterbury in devotion and practice. It serves to prove that Paul's admonition for the Corinthians is a relatively needless warning today since one may select his own mental reputation when he makes his selection of a church. Yet it ought to serve as a valid reminder that there is something to be gained by making our faith seem no more ludicrous than it need appear.

The Corinthians were not the last to make themselves seem needlessly uncollected. Christian tradition is filled with those who followed suit. St. Simeon Stylites, a "pillar saint," withdrew to the top of a post to live away from the tainted and the secular. In our day he would have been the frequent target of Halloween pranksters with air rifles. But in his own pre-BB era, he was simply called the "old fool on the pole." Of course, it is immediately obvious that many who saw him sitting up there month after month, rain or shine, would do everything they could to avoid Christianity. The assumption was that anyone who became a Christian would have to become a dimwitted aerialist too.

Earlier Christians often appeared less intelligent than they might have if they had managed to put into practice the saying that cleanliness is next to godliness. Since they considered nudity a sin, they also considered bathing a sin. Thus the most godly had an unforgettable aroma about them. Some wag further on in history remarked that they were possessed by "an odor of sanctity." As strange as it sounds, the greater their upwind proclivity, the more devout they were regarded to be.

St. Jerome wrote to St. Paula encouraging her not to tempt Satan by taking a bath. The advice may have been superfluous, since most of the "virgins" were so unkempt as to be tempting to no one, Satan notwithstanding. One of these early saints was cited for his supreme holiness by the fact that lice dripped from his body as he walked to worship. The sheer filth in which the faith of that time was incubated must have kept many away from the non-antiseptic madness called Christianity.

One particular order of nuns for decades of tradition always wore their robes while bathing. Their reason: "The Great God can see through bathroom walls." So, to appear decent before Him at all times, they took baths fully robed. Did they never see the illogic in their visualization of a God whose miraculous vision could pierce walls but not robes?

Fortunately, we have left behind these specific witnesses to our affair with madness. We are no longer unsanitary in our insanity. There are no pillar saints like Simeon. (I suspect, however, that there are still a good many Christians who prefer living a comfortable distance from corrupted hoi polloi.) Most distrust of the contemporary Christian mentality comes from more current eccentricities; these are as offensive to our generation as Simeon, Paula, and the ultramodest nuns were to theirs.

On one end of the philosophical spectrum are the conservative church groups and isms. Often these appear more unbalanced than they would if they were not characterized by certain affectations. For instance, witnessing — many church groups practice a type of armed missionaryism that scares the man on the street to death. Imagine his milieu: he lives routinely in the world of the Sane, but sometimes, suddenly, he is confronted with a Scripture-spouting churchman who has him by the throat and threatens him with hell. If he does not immediately accept the madness of the man who "has brought him the truth," he may be dismembered just outside the kingdom.

High churchmen, while never guilty of the curbstone attack, seem equally irrational when they demand of their parishioners unquestionable devotion to medieval dogma. Sometimes that dogma is so monstrous that to affirm a part of it would leave an unforgivable breach in even the novice's judgment. So, while Christianity may have matured over the past two thousand years, its fondness for the irrational has not greatly diminished.

The Sane have a twofold problem in seeking to evaluate the Mad. Simply put, they are suspicious and confused. Their suspicions come largely because they live outside the church; they do not therefore understand her sacraments or ordinances. They feed on hearsay: "Catholics believe Mary saves." "Presbyterians believe dancin' is a sin." "Lutherans are anti-Mason." "Baptists think they are the only ones going to heaven." "Methodists won't drink in front of each other." With only fragmentary gossip, they fit together the imagined creeds of most of the churches with which they are casually familiar. Knowing only enough to be suspicious of all, but not enough to come to faith in any, they live in confusion and doubt.

91

In the early decades of her development, the church of Jesus Christ was the object of Roman suspicion. The Romans didn't understand her. She had no buildings. She always met in rented halls or parks or catacombs and nearly always at night. The Romans heard that the Christians always talked about love; they assumed, therefore, since Christians always talked of love and met at night, that they carried on immoral practices. Further, they heard that these Christians always talked about the body and blood of Christ and thus they assumed that they secretly practiced cannibalism.

Being outside the church, the Romans sated their suspicions with gossip and hatred. So, when Rome burned, it might naturally be blamed on this new sect, illegal and insane — the Christians. They began to die for Roman sport, and for 250 years they were the whipping post of the emperors' frustrations. The Christians died because of their adherence to a kind of madness that the Romans could not understand.

In the same way, people outside the church in these present times are suspicious of doctrinarians and their rites because they have so little knowledge of them. Instead of seeking an understanding, it is far easier simply to dismiss the whole lot of churchmen as mad pietists.

Not only do their suspicions cause them to shy away from Christianity, but their confusion can afford them no rational place to begin a study of it. Many times I have tried to imagine myself outside of Christianity trying to decide if I wanted in. Who would I believe, Bishop Pike or Billy Graham? The Quakers or the Episcopalians? Would I prefer the Methodist softball team or the Baptist bowling league?

When I attempt to imagine myself on the outside of Christianity looking in, I confess I am hopelessly confused. To any sincere seeker outside Christ and His church, the whole kingdom of God must appear a madhouse without scheme or key. This may be the reason that the visiting guru is paraded through confetti and hailed as the messiah to those who are unsatisfied with their cold sanity and are seeking a more intelligible madness than Christianity appears to be.

Oddly enough, many who will call us madmen are those who wear our same name — Christian. There will be a qualitative difference in that name to the "nominal" Christian and to the person who lives in daily encounter with Christ.

It ought to be said that the "nominal" Christian will never refer to himself as "nominal." He rather prefers adjectives like "broad-minded, tolerant, teachable, open, discreet, moderate or let's-not-get-carried-away-with-it."

Doubtless the transcendence of the "Christian" Sane is not phenomenal to Christianity alone. Probably devout Buddhists are called "weirdos" by nominal Buddhists. Likewise, a progressive Jew of the Reformed Congregation might sneer at the quaint but fiery madness of an Orthodox rabbi.

Thus the worst kind of slurs occur between brothers. To hear men of the same label calling each other "fool" is painful. For any Christian to call another mad is to war against brotherhood in the kingdom of God. Yet it is done regularly. Jesus illustrated the seriousness of calling a brother "fool" when He said, "Whosoever shall say [to his brother], Thou fool, shall be in danger of hell fire" (Matt. 5:22).

But we who love Him and think Him supremely important must be prepared to live with even those labels given by our "Sane" brethren. Remember, He was given a few labels too: glutton, winebibber, prince of devils (in effect, madman).

Also, we know that our faith, though mysterious, does bring a full cup. We can endure the charges of deteriorated mentality for the sheer joy that has come upon us. Meaning and destiny must mean more to us than our reputation for injured sanity.

We are somehow like Legion (Luke 8:30ff), that pathetic figure of wild disorientation. Mad and untamed, fierce in his condition — Legion. Lights real, yet concocted by his fevered spasms, dived at him in soundless fury that no ears heard but his own. Not even his own ears really heard them; his mind alone heard and lied to his senses. His insanity imprisoned him in frenzy and drove him into wild, inhuman acts. His physique was brutish, which made him all the more unmanageable. He had actually broken chains during his storms of mania. Probably, when his seizures were over, his violence ended in sobbing like a tiny child for his pitiable condition. He was fierce and so was to be feared and, because he was feared, he was friendless. He lived alone, for he was violently mad.

Then this man meets Jesus the Christ. Christ is cautioned about his devastating seizures and his seething unpredictable tantrums. Their meeting is a lesson in redeeming peace. Suddenly this mad man is smiling into compassion, ultimate concern (to use Paul Tillich's term). The soul is swept clean by gentle eyes and a perfect mind. Those hands — yet unscarred — touch him, and the universe is instantly systematized. The strange world of "things" is no longer surging or threatening, but still and ordered. The lights which screamed and dived and frightened his boyish heart are gone, and the only light which remains is the sunlight playing on the strong, kind face of the Nazarene rabbi.

So he is clothed. Legion — mind you — clothed? He sits, perhaps, by the apostles' campfire and probes his

wonderful world of order. He smiles at Jesus with child-
ish adoration and laughs a free man's laughter. He
is a slate waiting to be chalked, to bear some message.
To walk among men and be one! This Christ has done
for him. To love a village child and be entrusted with
its safety was his ambition all the years of his madness.
Now he is whole, for Jesus has covered all his senseless
surgings with peace.

For so long I have longed for an epilogue to that
story, but Scripture does not hold it. It does say Legion
wished to be part of Jesus' retinue but was refused for
Jesus' own reasons. He did go about Decapolis telling
to all what great things Jesus had done for him. We
may guess part of the outcome, because many people
in every age have been skeptical about the miraculous
Christ.

We wonder what happened to Legion when he met
his first skeptic, as surely he did. We wonder at what
point in his radiant relationship with Christ he began
to realize that to many there had been no cure. To
many who heard his strange tale of peace and love,
Legion was yet mad. Someone inevitably told him that
he had traded his "diving lights" for a rabid and fanatic
infatuation. An intellectual of his day was sure to tell
the child-man, Legion, that his whole experience of
grace had been coincidental. A well-meaning apothecary
might have suggested a little post-trauma therapy. Sooner
or later Legion came to know that the Sane did not believe his tale of redemption. The part about the demons
going into the herd of swine was hard to swallow.
"Probably the whole herd was startled by desert thunder
and just stampeded about the same time you were
healed, Legion," they no doubt reasoned with him.

But, however they assessed his Christ-affliction, Legion
the enthusiastic madman, could not have minded. For

95

he had known both kinds of insanity, and he was in love with his new kind of affliction. Like Legion, we later believers find great meaning in our madness. It is because of that meaning that we even dare to be evangelistic with it. We are emboldened by the certainty of the substance over which we have been made stewards.

We are not presumptuous to feel that we have something to offer the Sane. We have felt pangs of compassion for their joyless sanity. We grant them their sanity when they insist we accept their evaluation of ours. But somehow they seem malnourished, and so, like lepers at a feast, we invite them to share our substance even if they believe it cankered. And because we believe we own so much, we may say what Kenneth Paatchen said in another context:

"Let us have madness openly, Oh, Men of my generation."

# CHAPTER SIX

ight half-believers of our casual creeds,
Who never deeply felt, nor clearly willed,
Whose insight never has borne fruit in deeds,
Whose vague resolves have never been fulfilled;

or whom each year we see
reeds new beginnings, disappointments new;
Who hesitate and falter life away,
And lose tomorrow the ground won today.

MATTHEW ARNOLD
The Scholar Gypsy

# NAKED IN THE DAY OF GRACE

THE owner of faith is a man of substance. No matter his capital assessment, he has means. Time and time again in the Scriptures the point is made. Which of the two from Jesus' parable is really wealthy, the tycoon Dives or the beggar Lazarus? Did not Jesus liken the kingdom of God to a treasure hid in the field? Indeed, He said that the Pearl of Great Price was earth's supreme value. If necessary, all should be sold to make possible its purchase. Paul called this precious faith "a treasure in an earthen vessel."

In lieu of this wealth attested in Scripture, why is it that the Christian appears intellectually and culturally impoverished? Grace has made us a people of substance, yet we are seen as disinherited refugees. Why in bounty do we seem deprived? Why, indeed, are we naked in the day of grace?

Besides the reasons examined in earlier chapters, there are other considerations worth observing. For instance: the phoniness of churchmen. To those outside the fold it seems that, while the insiders are initially drawn to church membership by the love of Christ, there soon develops a fondness for politics. The caucuses of the system are the coffee klatches and committee luncheons. And the most successful church politicians are those who, standing firmly on a platform of Christian humility, are able to become congregational moderator overnight. Many who get close enough to faith to get a good look at Christian bureaucracy are lost forever in the credibility gap that exists between our profession of love and our practice of utility.

Another face of our undoneness has been the vacuum which exists between the poles of social concern and pietism. Conservative evangelicals have often retreated from every appearance of social ministry. Sheer fear of the taint of humanism has kept them from being humanitarian. They have observed the truth of Dostoevsky that humanitarianism is the worst form of atheism. They have marked well that many who fix themselves on man's material woes never discover or heal man's spiritual woes. Thus they busy themselves in exegesis of the great evangelistic passages of the Bible and hastily read past Matthew 25:31-46 and James 2:15-17. Their fiery evangelism seems a quaint irrelevancy because it gets interested in only a few categories of human suffering. On the other hand, the liberals have severed completely their theological tether and have made for the ghettos of human suffering with generous servings of concern. The argument which has ensued between the camps has made us appear "wretched, and miserable, and poor, and blind, and naked" (Rev. 3:17).

Two other issues have caused the evangelical believer to appear a man without substance. First of all, the faithful often seem to live beyond culture. This criticism has usually been valid. While evangelicals busy themselves with prayer meetings, Bible studies, and worship services, many ignore theater, literature, and concerts. Many evangelicals who know the spirit of the great revival choruses have never seriously sampled Tchaikovsky or Beethoven or the current Broadway shows.

100

Most of them are not intentionally anti-Beethoven or anti-Bacharach; they just have not taken the time required for discovery. And because of this inadequacy among His disciples, Christ has sometimes appeared, to the cultured, an opponent of the fine arts. Christians have seemed culturally poor however vast their properties of faith.

In the second place, we evangelicals have often been stigmatized for our devotion to austerity. Our self-denial was frequently rigorous. Although there are many evidences now of a new, emerging liberality, our morality in the past was impelled by prohibitions often deemed excessive. Taboos are often the still observable marks of our piety. Christians once prided themselves that they were movie-less, tobacco-less, and poker-less. To those outside Christianity, the insiders were stingy with living. Believers seemed to have made themselves poor by tenderly fondling and stroking their thou-shalt-nots.

For these and other reasons, in the wealth of redeeming grace, we have sought like Adam to hide our nakedness. We have sung with fervor:

> My Father is rich in houses and lands,
> He holdeth the wealth of the world in his hand;
> Of rubies and diamonds, of silver and gold,
> His coffers are full, he has riches untold.
> I'm a child of the King. . . .

But our nakedness has been discovered. The skeptics have asked flippantly: "Christians have been around for two thousand years. Why, in two thousand years, could they not produce a world without the Gestapo and the Mafia? How much do you *really* own who call yourselves Christians?"

To answer their questions we must return to apology. The word "apology" comes from a Latin cognate *apo-*

101

*logia* which means "defense." Every Christian ought to be able to defend his substance. When the critics seek to expose our poverty, we should be able to demonstrate our great wealth in Christ. To succeed in making our own defense, several things are necessary.

First, we will have to move away from a purely devotional posture and embrace dialectic. A well-used cliché of conservatism is that one should "never argue over religion." Absurd! One should be prepared to argue with his life if necessary.

He who holds that religion is a purely devotional matter is negligent with love. Let us imagine a kindred situation:

A man is said to love his wife. He sees his wife as a respondent to his affections, a supplier of companionship, a complement to his loneliness. If someone in the marketplace suddenly degrades her with rude argument, he will only say, "I never argue about my wife. My wife is an object of devotion, not argument. Say what you will about her — I will not be embroiled in a debate over her."

As ridiculous as this sounds, this is the profile of the man who treasures his faith but will not defend it. There is no valid adoration of Christ that will not defend itself. There are moments when we look at our creeds with love and reverence. But there are also moments when we look at them protectively. If faith has any value, there will come bristling moments of defense when we will say like Luther, "Here I stand, I can do no other."

The second thing which we must do to make full proof of our convictions is to learn the philosophy of the opposition. This cannot be done by a sole focus on Scripture. The cynics usually subdue us because they know the Bible, plus a great deal more: art, philosophy,

102

and history. The evangelical Christian, conversely, knows only the Bible and too often has had only a surface knowledge of that. The ignorance of the devoted is perhaps the greatest threat to the Christian faith.

It is uncanny that, living in the era of the great explosion of knowledge, the average layman is reading very little and the average pastor only a little more. Unless we begin to read, our ignorance will not only make us incapable of defending our faith, it will relegate us to obscurity. This is a world of learning, of sight, sensation, and sound. Anything without nerve endings just cannot really belong. And when our cultural numbness has run its course, Christianity will be done for. Nothing animate ever lives for long after its nervous system has died.

Oh, how we need to discover our world! We need to read what it is thinking and feel where it is going. We need to know what the philosophers are saying, what the musicians are singing, and what the artists are painting, for only as we know our secular culture can we meet it head on. We have little time to lose in formulating an intelligent apology. We must know what the writers have been doing with the alphabet since the last time we used our library card.

Before we can argue defensively, we will have to recover our self-respect. We have lost it because we have heeded the liberal *detente*. In secular fields the liberals propagate, by premise or insinuation, their intellectual superiority. Instead of quietly accepting our inferiority, we need to study to erase that myth. In some cases the evangelical conservatives have viewed their equality. But many times they acquiesce. William Buckley's *Up From Liberalism* should be regarded a secular demonstration of our conservative self-esteem. Conservatism is not an intellectual stopover before the grand façade of liberal enlightenment. Conservatism may be a studied and intelligent way of life. But one thing is sure: the apologist who accepts his cultural inferiority will never manage a convincing defense of his substance.

Intellectual superiority has bitten and snapped at evangelicals even within Christianity. The high churchmen have looked at revivalism with scorn over the top of their gilded traditions. I'm sure that from time to time faithful Pentecostals must weary of hearing how many of the Presidents were Episcopalian.

In spite of the status wheel, the apologist must realize there are no second-class citizens in the kingdom of God. Conservative evangelicals are probably the only people with either the stamina or the message to change the world. They must, therefore, explore their own defense, rightfully accept it, and courageously enter into dialogue with their "elite" antagonists.

Like the heroes of the Alamo, we think we would feel safer if we fired back at our challengers from the inner sanctum of the church. But such is just not the case. Assuming that we have a healthy self-respect, let us with bravado take our case out of the church and state it in the marketplace.

Of course, there is a risk involved. Paul was not sure he would win his case on Mars Hill. He did, in fact, lose — but it was not a total loss. The openness of his debate had gained for Christ, Dionysius and Damaris and a few others (see Acts 17:34). Paul was an intellect, and the true intellect can never be really snubbed. The Athenian thinkers who had collided cerebrums with the apostle could not call him stupid. These Olympian religionists may have felt themselves superior to him, but their self-imposed superiority went without any demonstration.

The important issue was the openness of Paul's

104

apology. He had run the risk of open dialogue. Karl Jaspers is no doubt right when he says:

> If the churches dared . . . to put themselves in jeopardy, the Word would be credible everywhere, everyday, on the lips of priests and theologians. [1]

But we have not had the courage to risk the exposure. We have been too afraid of confirming the contention of the skeptic that we really are naked in the day of grace.

Our problem is severe. Not only have we been reluctant to try to defend our faith, most of the time we have refused even to acknowledge it. Before the believer has the strength to defend himself, he must at least develop the courage to speak up and acknowledge his substance. But even in a simple acknowledgment of Grace, he may feel naked and ashamed.

The story of the woman who had an issue of the blood ought to prod us into an overt stand. She touched Jesus in the press of the crowd and was healed by only the slightest contact with the hem of His garment. She had earnestly hungered for that brief contact that brought her healing. But she also enjoyed the anonymity of her contact; after touching Him, she tried to slip away amid the crowd without acknowledging that she had been healed. Yet Christ could not permit her that evasion of her responsibility: "Who touched me?" He asked.

In the anonymity of our healing He is surely still demanding, "Who touched me?" And if we regard that redemptive touch as a thing of great joy and worth, it is our responsibility to acknowledge our affair. And if we will seek the courage to acknowledge it, after we have matured in Christ, we will be able to defend it openly.

It is when the chips are down that we are the most fearful. Demas, Paul's beloved missionary friend, could not be brave because of the perilous risk of exposure. It is with pain that the apostle wrote, "Demas hath forsaken me, having loved this present world" (2 Tim 4: 10). The defense of the Gospel was fatal to Paul, and Demas was not up to that kind of pressure.

In the Dostoevsky novel about the famous Russian brothers, Ivan Karamazov is on the witness stand to testify in behalf of his brother, Dmitri, falsely convicted of the murder of his father. It was unfortunate that the strain under which Ivan had been living caused him to go mad at the critical moment of testimony. Although he was the only one in the courtroom with the knowledge to save Dmitri, his mind left him and he babbled incoherently as the issue was lost.

Perhaps the insane Ivan is the fearsome reflection of the Christian apologist. We have been asked by God to take the witness stand and bear our witness, for only the information that we have is able to save the world. So with trauma we do it. But our testimony often comes out garbled by personal experience and emotion and with no profound awareness of our predicament. Like the demented Ivan Karamazov, we are afraid to speak our apology to the aliens for fear of intellectual embarrassment.

Often we fail to make a substantial defense of faith for the sheer value of time. That is to say, in our harried occupation with the daily round, we do not see a little place to set apology in the crowd of important things which must be attended. This state of affairs shows how little we prize religious things. This posture is an admission that faith is a thing of small worth lost in the midst of all the really "big" things we do every day. There is simply no time to acknowledge or defend our belief. When we adopt this attitude, we deny faith by the precept that there is always time for what we really believe is of value.

Tolstoy wrote of the tendency to minimize faith by maximizing the routine involvements of living. He wrote in his now-famous *Memoirs of a Lunatic:*

> I well remember the second time madness seized me. It was when auntie was telling us about Christ. She told his story and got up to leave the room. But we held her back: "Tell us more about Jesus Christ!" we said. "I must go," she replied.
>
> "No, tell us more, please!" Mitinka insisted, and she repeated all that she had said before. She told us how they crucified him, how they beat and martyred him, and how he went on praying and did not blame them. "Auntie, why did they torture Him?"
>
> "They were wicked."
>
> "But wasn't he God?"
>
> "Be still — it is nine o'clock, don't you hear the clock striking?"
>
> "Why did they beat Him? He had forgiven them. Then why did they hit him? Did it hurt Him? Auntie, did it hurt?"
>
> Be quiet, I say, I am going to the dining room to have tea now."
>
> "But perhaps it never happened, perhaps he was not beaten by them?"
>
> "I am going!"
>
> "No, Auntie, don't go . . ." And again my madness took possession of me. I sobbed and sobbed, and began knocking my head against the wall. [2]

Young Tolstoy found it incomprehensible (if these memoirs are autobiographical, as many scholars believe) that Christ had been brutalized and his aunt was not interested enough to stay a little past tea-time to talk about it.

As a thing of value is never pre-empted by trivia, neither is real faith superseded by "tea-time." Anytime a believer allows a serious inquiry or even a challenge to pass unnoticed, he will communicate that his faith is of small value.

We must rise with the apology of meaning against the nihilism of our day. Nels F. S. Ferré observed:

> Modern man not only glories but grovels in despair. Nihilism is the style. All of a sudden the happy ending is taboo throughout the whole world of literature. [3]

The theologian's remark is reinforced by the nihilism of Federico Fellini, who wrote his world-view with these words:

> Like many people, I have no religion and I am just sitting in a small boat drifting with the tide. I live in the doubts of my duty. . . . I think there is dignity in this, just to go on working. . . . This is the way things are, you say, now what are we to do? Today we stand naked, defenseless, and more alone than at any time in history. We are waiting for something, perhaps another miracle, perhaps the Martians. Who knows? [4]

As we have already illustrated in another chapter, Christian meaning is set in opposition to nihilism. The tool with which we launch our offensive is our long-neglected apologetic. Unthreatened by the risk of losing, let us set forth our case.

We need also to bring our evidences of miracle against the growing tendency to "mechanize" Scripture event. Decades ago Harry Blamires foresaw the coming struggle of the new apologists with the dogmatic naturalists, and he wrote of the conflict:

> . . . between those who give full weight to the supernatural reality at the heart of all Christian dogma, practice and thought, and those who try to convert Christianity into a naturalistic religion by whittling away the reality and comprehensiveness of its supernatural basis. [5]

Perhaps the day he envisioned is here. We must meet the moment of defense prepared.

To make our apology effective, we must learn to distinguish between the flippant skeptic and the seeking skeptic. "God is dead!" has been said with two distinct intonations. T. J. J. Altizer seemed to be saying it in the arrogant, academic flippancy of his fledgling professorship; maybe there was a discreet joy he harbored for stirring fur in the Bible Belt — like a mischievous boy salting snails on a hot sidewalk.

But there is another way it has been said: "God is dead, but I sincerely wish he were not. How I hunger just one time to cry out in a senseless world, 'The Lord is my Shepherd, I shall not want.'" Hungering unbelief is always capable of redemption. In truth, the hungering unbelief is nearly always hungering belief in disguise. Wherever it is found is the place for compassionate apology.

An effective defense will always do two things. First, it will cause the unbeliever to examine his position. Caution is needed here. Any attempt on the part of the apologist to imply, "You must not have thought very much about your position, or you couldn't possibly believe that," is snobbery. (Let the evangelicals remember that not all intellectual snobbery comes from the agnostics.) Still, while we are seeking to get someone to examine Christianity for the first time, he may progress faster if he is allowed to re-examine the values he already holds.

The apologist needs to be considerate enough to listen to all the skeptics' views, however far out they may seem. Listening is compassionate, and the doubter must see the apologist as a "big ear" and not a "big mouth." Many an apology was finished by the Christian's impatience for conversion. Many have ended when the believer's intolerance of agnosticism caused him to blurt out: "That's the dumbest thing I ever heard!"

Others who might have believed were thwarted by Christian naïveté. Some evangelicals feel that if only the skeptic would "accept Christ," all his doubts would pass away. So, in the midst of a discussion of the unreasonableness of the virgin birth, we divert the discussion to "The Four Spiritual Laws" or the "Roman Road to Salvation." The reversing of the cart and horse makes the whole dialectic so unwieldy that the skeptic abandons the conversation as a useless attempt to counter fanaticism.

If the apologist argues convincingly, he must not be afraid to lose. No one likes a poor sport. The tendency, when backed into a corner by good debaters, is to retreat behind pious churchmanship and bland clichés. The argument is not lost, for it is usually continuable if the Christian ends by saying, "I'll think about that!" It is dead with no chance of resurrection after a pious clincher, "I'll pray about it, dear brother, and trust God!" Any fight is more admired if it ends with naked fists. And if there has even been a serious examination of ideas, it is triumph of a kind.

The second thing an effective defense will do is compel the opponent to live with the consequences of his decision. For a long time the methodology of wit-

110

ness has been to draw alternatives, then ask for a decision. The apologist dealing with the skeptic ought to use the same methods. Often, during the defense of faith, the alternatives tend to "fuzz up," and both the meaning and the consequence of the choice are obscured. The very nature of doubt is indecision. Therefore, often the sincere and seeking doubter may appear to be moving in the direction of faith logically and progressively when, all of a sudden, he blurts out his honest misgivings about belief and the whole objective may be derailed for a while. It may be derailed for a long time.

But wherever possible the apologist ought to seek a summary to the encounter. And the summary of the dialogue should clearly mark the route the decision must take. The decision may carry the doubter in the direction of faith or it may confirm him in his agnosticism — these should be pointed out. Further, there exists the possibility that the doubter may not be advancing in either direction but merely living in frustration at the fork of the road. The consequences of that frustration may be mentally splintering, for indecision is a peaceless and despair-ridden state of being.

The importance of the defense of faith is paramount in the current day of doubt. The best argument for the legitimacy of belief will always be offered by those who are really convinced that their spiritual holdings are major resources for living and dying. Salvation is a treasure indeed. When it is so regarded, it is spontaneously defended. As Christopher Morley said in *Kitty Foyle*, "Nobody knows what he really believes, you've got to guess at it by how you find yourself acting." Those who find themselves reacting spontaneously against aggressive doubt may be assured of their substance. In lieu of this, let us defend the Pearl of Great Price with the determination of the martyrs.

111

The Scriptures have warned us of a time when "many shall follow their pernicious ways; by reason of whom the way of truth shall be evil spoken of" (2 Peter 2:2).

On the contrary, let us make Paul's counsel to the slaves our own:

> Let as many servants as are under the yoke count their own masters worthy of all honour, that the name of God and his doctrine be not blasphemed (1 Tim. 6:1).

# CHAPTER SEVEN

Goliath may prosper but David will prevail.

ANTHONY TOWNE
*Excerpts from the Diaries*

# EXIT THE WITCHES

DOUBT is a demoralizer. Regarding the church and her faith, the attack has been full scale. No matter how much the faithful steel themselves against it, it is difficult for it not to have some effect.

Let us say that after breakfast, which has been preceded by Bible reading and prayer, we pick up the paper to read the now famous headlines:

## GOD IS DEAD IN GEORGIA

EMINENT DEITY SUCCUMBS DURING
SURGERY; SUCCESSION IN DOUBT
AS ALL CREATION GROANS

### President Orders Flags at Half Staff

And the first line of copy runs, "God, creator of the universe . . . died late yesterday during major surgery undertaken to correct a massive diminishing influence." Such sensational satire might not visibly affect us.

But suppose, as we look on down the endless row of copy, we see another article back near the church page: *Computer Predicts Denominational Decease!* The substance of this article is that the United Presbyterian Church is dying at least numerically. Some religious technicians, noticing the decline in membership year by year, programmed a computer to deal with the trend.

115

One of the computer's discoveries was that, based on present trends of membership loss, the superdenomination would baptize its last baby in the spring of 1991. Breakfast is unaffected. The compound negative of the death of God and the death of the church is passed by without a stir of reaction.

Then, on the way to work, the car radio blares a wire-service release: the skeleton of an extremely intelligent Jew has been discovered during excavation in Jerusalem's ancient temple area; there are evidences that the victim died of crucifixion. The implications of this third news release are quite obvious and fix a strange negativity into our day.

It is not as though we have ceased to be a people of faith, but there is an emerging, grave dread that accompanies us wherever we go. It is reinforced by articles, movies, books, lines from the theater. Why, all of a sudden, does the minister's name on the confirmation certificate look like a forgery? What is this alien, unsettled feeling that truth is all at once bogus?

We reassure ourselves with a Scripture text on the endurance of the church: "The gates of hell shall not prevail against it" (Matt. 16:18). And we know, as we have always known, that God is not dead — not even sick — and only the "fool hath said in his heart, There is no God" (Ps. 14:1). Is it possible that the negativism of our day is getting to us? If not, why in spite of these promises are we apprehensive in the presence of the philosophers?

The strange new impudence of the secular thinkers is intimidating us. Erich Segal's lovers (in *Love Story*) are atheists but live for a while at least in resplendent meaning. Thus we see them doing on the screen what we say cannot be done; they are living meaningfully without Christ.

Or, there is Her Militancy, Mrs. Madelyn Murray O'Hair, threatening us when we say the Lord's Prayer or read the Bible on space shots, or protesting nativity sets in front of government buildings at Christmas time. While it is true that we think of her as a radical departure from the norm, the norm seems less secure because of her. Bertrand Russell posited agnosticism so logically that his defense of it makes all but the firmest disciples feel a momentary chill of uncertainty.

In J. D. Salinger's *Franny and Zooey*, the impudence is just plain snide. Franny, who is about to have a nervous breakdown, has turned in her insecurity to religion and Jesus. (This alone is enough to say that only the insecure need it.) Franny also has a propensity for cheeseburgers. Her mother, a chicken-soup supporter, intimates that Franny's improper diet (the cheeseburgers) may be the reason for her fanaticism. Zooey comes right out and expresses what to most of us would be sacrilege; to his mother he says:

> Do you realize what you've done? You've given this whole . . . issue a fresh, new Biblical slant. I wrote four papers in college on the Crucifixion — five, really — and every one of them worried me half crazy because I thought something was missing. Now I know what it was. Now it's clear to me. I see Christ in an entirely different light. His unhealthy fanaticism. His rudeness to those nice, sane, conservative, tax-paying Pharisees. Oh, this is exciting! In your simple, straightforward, bigoted way, Bessie, you've sounded the missing keynote to the whole New Testament. Improper diet. Christ lived on cheeseburgers and Cokes. For all we know, he probably fed the mult . . . [1]

Imbedded in literature ever so subtly is the snare by which we are subconsciously drawn into doubt.

117

For instance, the movie of 1971, McCabe and Mrs. Miller, takes place in a little town called Presbyterian Church. The town is famous for every kind of moral excess that an "R" rating will allow a film. The church is only incidental to life and morality until it catches on fire, and then the town joins in the fight to save it. The message left with the theatergoer is the utter irrelevancy of the church.

Thus step by step we strengthen our doubts about the faith and the church. Even titles of books like The Last Years of the Church by David Poling insinuate that the church is done for. Our decay seems so utter that when the Beatles say they are more popular than Jesus, the statement meets only token resentment. Aldous Huxley in Brave New World pictures a time when the churches have lopped the top off the crosses which adorned them so that every church proudly wears a new "T" instead. The "T" stands for Henry Ford and the automobile era (Model T Ford), when man had come to admire and even worship his own technical genius.

Examples like all of these are abundant. Is the church dying? Will the faith "once delivered unto the saints" (Jude 3) be superseded by something more acceptable to the tomorrow which is already banging at our doors? How great a threat is this coming age to the present worship?

Doubts never erase easily and, while they stand, our aptitude for convincing others of our security is practically nil. In concluding the book, therefore, let me mention three things which must be accomplished if we are to drive out the witches of doubt. Not only must they all be accomplished, but they must all be held in equal reverence and carried out with the same zeal.

First of all, we must learn our creeds. It is quixotic to try to defend what we do not understand. An argument from weakness is a losing position. Of course, knowing our creed means knowing the Bible. Our ignorance in this area is causing us to be pushed back by the advance of the skeptics. In a recent survey given to "steadfast" laymen who were long-time church members, the results were most revealing. Some thought "epistles" were the wives of "apostles"! Most could not name four of the apostles. The great words of faith were indefinable to most: Incarnation, Atonement, Transfiguration.

The apostle Paul admonished Timothy to "study to shew thyself approved" (2 Tim. 2:15). Perhaps the admonition of the apostle to the Christians of today would be "Study to survive!" It is naive to think we can quit thinking. Ignorance in any field of learning in this day of intense education will in a short time see that field pass away. Christianity has never seen an acceptable day for "dummies," and it never will.

We are prone to step up emotionalism (especially in the evangelical churches) while we gear down intellectually. We learn rather quickly that "feeling" is a more automatic attribute of faith than knowledge. It is easier to make our worship services a joyful binge than a serious classroom. Theology is the skeletal system upon which Christendom supports itself. Because this is true, it is unthinkable that we have felt it too "scientific" to be of practical consequence in our lives. Let it be understood: joy without understanding is bilious and short-lived in the face of any crisis.

Let us remember, too, that the followers of Jesus were and are called "disciples." The word means "student." Calling oneself a disciple indicates that one is involved in a study of the Man and His teachings. The average parent, when he sends his child off to school in the fall, wants the child to apply himself. The idea of his child becoming a truant when everything valuable depends upon education is unthinkable. Most disciples are not truant, although more and more are missing church as a habitual way of life. But most are attending church without learning. The tragedy of the modern church is that, with thousands of dollars tied up in buildings and supplies, little coordinated and serious learning is taking place.

The Hebrew faith has endured centuries of privation and martyrdom in dispersion. The reason for the Jews' survival is tied up in their tradition and their education. Unfortunately, Protestantism is relatively young and has few long-standing traditions. As our education becomes weaker and weaker, we lose a great deal of the resilience needed to stand against the winds of the new technocracy. We must learn thoroughly and learn fast.

Unless we know what a Christian is, we have no right to call ourselves Christian. The statement may be extended to the various denominations. Can an unstudied man call himself a Baptist? Does not a Methodist have to know what his credo claims before he can call himself by the creed?

The church must catch the New Testament view of herself once again. Many "Christians" basically see themselves as "attenders." Witness how frequently one hears the question, "Where do you go to church?" Never is the question phrased, "At what church are you a student?" Always the question goes, "How long have you been a Presbyterian?" and never, "How long have you been a disciple?" The synagogue has always seen itself as the hub of Jewish education. The church has rather viewed herself as the "rally" house. Her invitation has always been "Come feel with me" and rarely "Come learn with me."

The current popularity of small-group Bible studies

may point to a widespread hunger to know more than the church has been teaching. One thing is certain: to know little is to feel unsure of oneself. In this frame of mind, we are not likely to enter into a serious defense of faith and are unlikely to win if we do. Doubt is a destructive witch, and the only way to drive her out is to become a serious student of our tenets.

Second in importance to knowing our creed is our acceptance of it. This acceptance must be wholehearted. The defense of a creed can never be more confident than its endorsement by the mind of the believer. A salesman unconvinced about the value of his product cannot expect to be very successful.

It is an inevitable principle of sales that confidence in the product produces self-confidence in the sales presentation. If this sounds like religious "Dale Carnegie-ism," be assured the principle is indeed valid. One can imagine the apostle Paul's weakness in his critical defense before Nero if he had suffered an attack of doubt. Rather, knowing that the Gospel of Christ was "the power of God unto salvation" (Rom. 1:16), the confidence of that Gospel produced the kind of confidence in him that empowered him to stand alone and to say:

> At my first answer no man stood with me, but all men forsook me: I pray God that it may not be laid to their charge. Notwithstanding the Lord stood with me, and strengthened me; that by me the preaching might be fully known, and that all the Gentiles might hear: and I was delivered out of the mouth of the lion (2 Tim. 4:16, 17).

Paul's martyrdom after his final stand is almost certain. Martyrdom points to an essential aspect of our argument for faith. The argument is more important than the person who bears it. The argument actually adorns the bearer. This is certainly true in purely academic areas. For instance, when I hear the name "Marx," I do not immediately think of his picture; I think of his arguments — the *Manifesto, Das Kapital,* and the rest. Only if I think long enough may I see the faint outlines of his image. Then I recall that he was bearded, high of brow, and possessed with wide-set, deep and piercing eyes.

The same goes for Paul of Tarsus. He is not an image. Oh, if we think a moment we may recall the general impressions of the painters and novelists: shortened frame, hunched back, bald pate. But that image emerging from sheer imagination is secondary or tertiary to *the* Paul. It is his argument we remember. Not only does it adorn his person; it has become his person.

This is Paul: First and Second Corinthians, Romans, the Prison Letters. This is Paul:

> And I, brethren, when I came to you, came not with excellency of speech or of wisdom, declaring unto you the testimony of God. For I determined not to know anything among you, save Jesus Christ, and him crucified (1 Cor. 2:1,2).

Paul is an Argument, determined and sure of itself, accepting fully each of its analyzed doctrines.

His studied certainty had driven out the witches of doubt. He is never found saying: "For to me to live is Christ *I think*" (Phil. 1:21). Or, "God was *probably* in Christ reconciling the world unto himself" (2 Cor. 5:19). No, his was a certain trumpet proclaiming in assurance: "I know whom I have believed" (2 Tim. 1:12).

People die, but arguments live. They argue for centuries after those are gone who first declared them.

And it is a fascinating thing to watch a modern cynic slashing at the arguments of a dead man. The argument slashes back. Paul is not a dead argument, only a dead man. And the late Lord Russell, with all his brilliance, twenty centuries after the fact is in debate with Paul, a first century letter writer. And the debate with Paul is serious enough to muster first-rate publications by the philosopher, sternly setting agnosticism against grace. But Paul is still selling more copies of Romans than Russell is *Why I Am Not a Christian*, let us say. And Paul's argument, as some poet said, is rather like an anvil wearing out hammers along the corridors of history and doubt. Paul knew and accepted his creed, and his argument was not dissolved by time.

One further force is important in driving doubt from our view of Scripture. We must begin to live our creed. No creed is merely of meditational value. It is at the point of creedal action where Christianity is most in danger of being lost. Back to Marx for an illustration: suppose Communists met one day a week and repeated the Communist Manifesto, sang hymns about it, and had a sermon on it. Then suppose they went out to live like Republicans or Tsarists or Capitalists. The Communists are a threat to the West because they are "creed-dwellers."

It is easier by far to argue with creedal thinking than it is to argue with creedal living. Consider what inconsistent living has done to build hypocrisy into the Apostles' Creed: "I believe in God the Father Almighty . . ." but see myself as sovereign and self-directed. "I believe that Christ rose from the dead . . ." sort of, "and that He is seated at the right hand of the Father in heaven . . ." although the Russian cosmonauts have me wondering about that, too; "From whence he shall come . . ." That's far-fetched, isn't it? I mean

123

Jesus coming just as Matthew and Billy Graham always talk about. It is unthinkable. When a great creed becomes incidental to our practice, the skeptics have a better than average chance of burying our faith.

No wonder that the poet has rhymed our "thumb-worn Creeds" with our "large professions and our little deeds." And remember James's admonition: "Be ye doers of the word (the creed), and not hearers only, deceiving your own selves" (James 1:22). James says the creed is valueless when it divides affirmation from practice: "Thou believest that there is one God; thou doest well: the devils also believe" (James 2:19). Perhaps the greatest insecurity to the hypocrite ought to be the confrontation of this fact: the devil is a believer! But he is not a convincing apologist because his belief is so incidental to his practice.

Creed-living not only authenticates Christianity for the unbeliever but, practiced consistently, will gradually push back the confining doubts that surround the believer and will grant him a new day of freedom. Living a philosophy is substance. Thinking one is vaporous.

The answer, odd as it may sound, means that we must handle our philosophies when our hands are full. Yes, in the press of doing other things, we must handle our creeds, too. Remember the fable about the little engine who puffed with certainty, "I think I can . . . I know I can . . ." as he steamed and chortled his way up the grade? He might have hissed the discussion in the railyards with other academic engines and never known the joy of a functional creed. But on the slopes it was different! While he strained at the creed in an effort to make it work, his success was fixed by the demonstration.

I once knew a great miler whose credo was: "No one is ever too tired to take the next step." How many times he had employed this in time trials one could not guess. Forty steps from the finish tape he knew he could take step thirty-nine; at step thirty-nine he knew he could manage step thirty-eight, and so on until the race was won. The reality of his creed had been tried in the "crunch" of the cinder track. He knew it worked.

Doing our doctrine is always the death of doubt. When Paul was first called into Christianity, he was uncertain, crying out: "Who art thou, Lord?" (Acts 9:5). But at the end he confirmed convictions that had been tried by every adversity and exclaimed in confidence: "I know whom I have believed. . . . Henceforth there is laid up for me a crown of righteousness, which the Lord, the righteous judge, shall give me at that day" (2 Tim. 1:12; 4:8). Confidence always comes by immersing creed in circumstance.

Learning and accepting and living our creed will result in a mature confidence. The mature Christian is probably the best argument for convincing the unbeliever. Doubt cannot live with this maturity: they are alien bedfellows. When certitude comes in, the doubts must go. In the process of this growing, we become unafraid to love and live our argument openly for we know we are a people of substance.

It is somehow like witches that plagued our childhood. Remember them? They lurked in the flowery print of darkened wallpaper. They huddled in the shadows of an open closet door. They shrieked in the howl and circumstance of a fierce electrical storm. But as we grew up we saw less and less of them. Then, somehow, they were gone, and we were grown and unafraid.

# FOOTNOTES

CHAPTER 2

1 Vance Packard, *The Waste Makers*. (New York: David McKay, 1960), pp. 277-78.

2 Charles A. Reich, *The Greening of America*. (New York: Dell, 1971), p. 334.

3 Adam Smith, *The Money Game*. (New York: Dell, 1969), p. 80.

4 Elton Trueblood, *Company of the Committed*. (New York: Harper & Row, 1961), p. 15.

CHAPTER 3

1 Lewis Mumford, *The Myth of the Machine*. (New York: Harcourt Brace Jovanovich, 1970), p. 430.

2 C. S. Lewis, *Miracles*. (New York: Association Press, 1958), pp. 39-40.

3 Bill Bright, *Revolution Now*. (San Bernardino, CA: Campus Crusade for Christ, Inc., 1969), p. 15.

4 Malcolm Muggeridge, *Jesus Rediscovered*. (New York: Doubleday, 1969), p. 147.

5 Virgil, *Virgil's Works, The Aeneid, Eclogues, Georgics*, trans. J. W. Mackail. (New York: Random House, 1950), pp. 274-75.

6 Amos Wells, as quoted in William Barclay, *And He Had Compassion on Them*. (Edinburgh: The Church of Scotland Youth Committee, 1955), pp. 106-7.

CHAPTER 4

1 Viktor Frankl, *Man's Search for Meaning*. (New York: Washington Square Press, 1963), p. 155.

2 Albert Camus, *The Fall*. (New York: Random House, 1956), p. 133.

3 Frankl, *op. cit.*, p. 160.

[4] From Henry Miller's *Tropic of Cancer,* quoted by H. R. Rookmaaker, *Modern Art and the Death of a Culture.* (Downers Grove, Ill.: Inter-Varsity Press, 1970), p. 146.

[5] Quoted by Rookmaaker, *Modern Art,* p. 145.

[6] Helen Keller, *The Story of My Life.* (Garden City: Doubleday, Doran and Co., 1936), pp. 23-24.

CHAPTER 6

[1] Martin E. Marty, *Varieties of Unbelief.* (Garden City: Doubleday, 1966), p. 211.

[2] *The Existential Imagination,* edited by Frederick Karl and Leo Hamilton. (New York: Fawcett, 1963), pp. 75-76.

[3] Nels F. S. Ferre, *The Finality of Faith.* (New York: Harper & Row, 1963), p. 6.

[4] Quoted by M. V. C. Jeffreys, *Personal Values in the Modern World.* (Baltimore: Penguin, 1962), p. 9.

[5] Elton Trueblood, *New Man for Our Time.* (New York: Harper & Row, 1970), p. 124.

CHAPTER 7

[1] J. D. Salinger, *Franny and Zooey.* (New York: Bantam, 1961), p. 86.